LONGMAN LITERATURE

POEMS 1

CW01471970

Editor: Celeste Flower

LONGMAN

Longman Literature

Series editor: Roy Blatchford

Novels

Jane Austen   *Pride and Prejudice*   0 582 07720 6
Charlotte Brontë   *Jane Eyre*   0 582 07719 2
Emily Brontë   *Wuthering Heights*   0 582 07782 6
Anita Brookner   *Hotel du Lac*   0 582 25406 X
Marjorie Darke   *A Question of Courage*   0 582 25395 0
Charles Dickens   *A Christmas Carol*   0 582 23664 9
                          Great Expectations   0 582 07783 4
                          Hard Times   0 582 25407 8
George Eliot   *Silas Marner*   0 582 23662 2
F Scott Fitzgerald   *The Great Gatsby*   0 582 06023 0
                          Tender is the Night   0 582 09716 9
Nadine Gordimer   *July's People*   0 582 06011 7
Graham Greene   *The Captain and the Enemy*   0 582 06024 9
Thomas Hardy   *Far from the Madding Crowd*   0 582 07788 5
                          The Mayor of Casterbridge   0 582 22586 8
                          Tess of the d'Urbervilles   0 582 09715 0
Susan Hill   *The Mist in the Mirror*   0 582 25399 3
Aldous Huxley   *Brave New World*   0 582 06016 8
Robin Jenkins   *The Cone-Gatherers*   0 582 06017 6
Doris Lessing   *The Fifth Child*   0 582 06021 4
Joan Lindsay   *Picnic at Hanging Rock*   0 582 08174 2
Bernard Mac Laverty   *Lamb*   0 582 06557 7
Jan Mark   *The Hillingdon Fox*   0 582 25985 1
Brian Moore   *Lies of Silence*   0 582 08170 X
Beverley Naidoo   *Chain of Fire*   0 582 25403 5
                          Journey to Jo'burg   0 582 25402 7
George Orwell   *Animal Farm*   0 582 06010 9
Alan Paton   *Cry, the Beloved Country*   0 582 07787 7
Ruth Prawer Jhabvala   *Heat and Dust*   0 582 25398 5
Paul Scott   *Staying On*   0 582 07718 4
Virginia Woolf   *To the Lighthouse*   0 582 09714 2

Short Stories

Jeffrey Archer   *A Twist in the Tale*   0 582 06022 2
Thomas Hardy   *The Wessex Tales*   0 582 25405 1
Susan Hill   *A Bit of Singing and Dancing*   0 582 09711 8
George Layton   *A Northern Childhood*   0 582 25404 3
Bernard Mac Laverty   *The Bernard Mac Laverty Collection*   0 582 08172 6

Poetry

Five Modern Poets   edited by Barbara Bleiman   0 582 09713 4
Poems from Other Centuries   edited by Adrian Tissier   0 582 22595 X
Poems in My Earphone   collected by John Agard   0 582 22587 6
Poems 1   edited by Celeste Flower   0 582 25400 0
Poems 2   edited by Paul Jordan & Julia Markus   0 582 25401 9

Other titles in the Longman Literature series are listed on page 174.

Contents

CONTENTS

Charles Causley   36

About the poet   36

Grace Nichols   58

About the poet   58

CONTENTS

John Betjeman   72

About the poet   72

Elizabeth Jennings   91

About the poet   91

CONTENTS

Wendy Cope   107

About the poet   107

Gillian Clarke   122

About the poet   122

CONTENTS

Introduction

Where to begin

Enjoy it! This is exactly where to begin with poetry. Poetry is meant to be heard and we should all try to read it aloud, and listen to others reading it as often as possible.

Although we do not realise it, we have all been learning about poetry since the day of our birth. None of us remembers the very first words we spoke, but they are likely to have been poetry. 'Mama' or 'Dada' or 'Papa' or 'Nana' – all of these words have an *internal rhyme* (words in bold italics are explained in 'Technical terms' on pages 144–8). Although they are not poems in themselves, these words are firm proof that the sounds and patterns language can make come as first nature to us all.

Before too long we really begin to enjoy the patterns of poetry. As toddlers, with our relatives and friends, we sing and chant nursery rhymes. We accompany our skipping, and tag and ball games, with songs and chants. The sounds of the words and the rhythms they set up are as important as the words themselves. **Rhymes** and rhythms (or beats as in music) help us remember what the next part of the game is, the next line or verse of the chant and the next action.

Poetry all around us

When we reach the age at which we no longer sing or recite nursery rhymes or join in playground games, we don't leave poetry behind. Quite the contrary. When I go to a football match and join in with the chanting and clapping of the crowd I am making poetry – poetry with clear rhythms and rhymes. If the chant we sing is based on an old folk song or a new pop song we could well be creating a *parody* or a *pastiche*. If I chant disparaging or jokey things about a player on the opposition team I could be indulging in lampoon (a form of scathing poem which makes fun of people). If I sing great things about the hero of the team I support I am probably creating a eulogy, or poem of praise.

If this all sounds a little far-fetched, and I want to prove to you how widespread poetry is in our lives, all you need to do is turn on the television. When 'Beanz Meanz . . .' there's a rhyme to answer for it, and your Super Sexy Sensational Sunday News would be nowhere without *alliteration*. Advertisers recognise the power of poetry to get inside your head. They know that it's easy to remember and recite. It can make us smile and can jog our memories about quite unrelated things, with its power of association. We enjoy the sound of poetry, the cleverness of its language and style, and the advertisers enjoy its selling power.

Subconscious poetry

That's not all. Whether we realise it or not we are all using poetry in our everyday speech. Now I believe that I usually speak in a down-to-earth and factual way, yet I cannot avoid using *figurative language* however hard I try. When my Great Aunt Agatha suggests that my sister and I are 'like two peas in a pod' I want to protest. She's not as good-looking as I am! Nevertheless, Auntie's *simile* makes sense to me. I decide to retaliate. 'She's a frog!', I reply, using a *metaphor* (which my sister would claim was grossly exaggerated). Perhaps you now have a good *image* in your minds of how she looks.

One thing we will realise through the poems in this anthology is the enormous variety of subjects, themes and styles. Poets write about everything around them and they suit the style of the writing to the *subject matter* and *theme*. They make fun of serious subjects at times or treat something funny with a note of sarcasm. The main thing we as readers of poetry must remember is to listen out for the voice behind the words. Often the best way to do this is to read the words out for ourselves. Which brings us back to where we started.

Reading the poems

Beginning to study poetry is an exciting process, but one that needs time. It is never enough to read a poem once, nor even just twice. Poems need savouring. They need to be listened to and they need to be looked at time and time again. Here then is the way to make the study and enjoyment of poetry work.

1. Choose your area of study. You could read all the poems by one poet or just some of them. Or you could select poems written by different poets that have something in common (see pages 170–2 for some ideas).

2. Make sure that you have copies of the poems. Read them quietly to yourself at least once. Then read them aloud, sharing them out if you can. Everyone should have an opportunity to read something, particularly if it is a poem, or part of one, that they have enjoyed.

3. Next, on your own or with others, make notes in a notebook on your early impressions of each poem. If there are words or phrases that you do not understand, make a note of them. (Some of them are explained in the Glossary.) Write down any questions you may have about the poem's subject or ideas.

4. Share your queries, and your answers, with the rest of the class and with your teacher, a poem at a time. You may need to research things in your library, or look words up in a dictionary, before you have a complete feel for what the poet is saying to you. Keep re-reading the poems too. Each time you read, things will become clearer.

When you are sure you understand the subject matter and ideas behind the poem fully, you need to take your study of poetry a step further. Ask yourself this question:

- Why did the writer use *poetry* to make their point or give this description, when they could have used ordinary prose?

The short answer is that the poet believes that the **form** and style of writing he or she uses somehow *enhances* what they have to say, making it more vivid and memorable. How do we recognise the style and the form?

5 Look at the poems, searching for patterns (**rhyme schemes**, long and short lines, number of lines in a **stanza**, etc.). Patterns often stand out clearly on the page. Ask yourself if the arrangement of the words reminds you of anything or visually helps you understand more about the words.

6 Listen to the poems. Try to hear patterns (rhyme schemes again, repeated letters and sounds, strong beats or rhythms).Does the poem dance, lilt, lollop, or process like a stately funeral? How does the movement of the poem suit its subject matter or theme? Ask yourself whether the sounds made affect how you feel about the words or help you to speak them.

7 Look again at the words. Samuel Taylor Coleridge wrote that poetry is 'the best words in the best order'. Poets make deliberate choices about words so that we find ourselves listening to them more carefully.

Gillian Clarke tells us that a pregnant cow's belly is a 'deep cathedral'. Of course it is not really any such thing, but by using this metaphor she brings the ideas of hugeness, darkness and even reverence to the image of the cow. In the same poem ('The Vet') she describes the birth of the calf, which slithers from its mother 'furled in a waterfall'. She has been told by the vet in the poem that watching the birth 'won't be pleasant', yet the poet's description gives the event an unexpected grace and beauty. She shows us the new-born calf using a simile: it 'swam home like a salmon . . . gleaming, silver sweet'. Suddenly we have to think hard about the comparison. It's a pleasant surprise because it can tell us a lot about the event; we just need to associate the ideas in our heads with the poet's unusual way of thinking.

The words are not there by chance so you need to question the choices: what difference does it make if you hear an owl cry or hear it scream?

8 Take a third look at the words, this time concentrating on their arrangement. The 'best order' for words needs to be carefully thought out. Poets often deliberately write sentences which sound out-dated if they want to make their poem sound older. Charles Causley wrote:

> 'O never shall young Edgcumbe
>   Bow or bend the knee
> Or speak or sing "Long live the King"
>   To such a man as he.'

Put this into everyday prose and you will realise how different the **syntax** (or word-order) of poetry can be.

Where words appear in the lines makes a difference to the stress or emphasis put upon them, particularly when they appear at the start of a line or occupy a whole line or sentence of their own. Look at Liz Lochhead's 'Favourite Shade' to see how effective a single word like 'Dreich', or even just 'Black', can become, because of where it is placed in the line.

9 Listen again to the poems. This time try to picture in your head what is happening. How sharp are the pictures? Are any of these images unusual or unexpected? If something is described as if it resembles another thing, does the comparison actually help to form an even clearer picture in your head?

The Study programme (pages 149–73) suggests ways into the poems in this anthology, and activities and projects based around them. Your next step could be to refer to it. Nevertheless, whether you are asked to talk or write about poetry, if you follow the steps above you will find you are able to do so confidently. Read, listen, question, discuss.

Commenting on a poem: *Jabberwocky*

'Twas brillig, and the slithy toves
    Did gyre and gimble in the wabe:
All mimsy were the borogoves,
    And the mome raths outgrabe.

'Beware the Jabberwock, my son!
    The jaws that bite, the claws that catch!
Beware the Jubjub bird, and shun
    The frumious Bandersnatch!'

He took his vorpal sword in hand:
    Long time the manxome foe he sought –
So rested he by the Tumtum tree,
    And stood awhile in thought.

And, as in uffish thought he stood,
    The Jabberwock, with eyes of flame,
Came whiffling through the tulgey wood,
    And burbled as it came!

One, two! One, two! And through and through
    The vorpal blade went snicker-snack!
He left it dead, and with its head
    He went galumphing back.

'And, hast thou slain the Jabberwock?
    Come to my arms, my beamish boy!
O frabjous day! Callooh! Callay!'
    He chortled in his joy.

'Twas brillig, and the slithy toves
    Did gyre and gimble in the wabe:
All mimsy were the borogoves,
    And the mome raths outgrabe.

Lewis Carroll

When Alice, in her travels through the looking-glass, read this poem, she had this to say about it: 'It seems very pretty, but it's *rather* hard to understand! . . . Somehow it seems to fill my head with ideas – only I don't know what they are! However, *somebody* killed *something*: that's clear, at any rate – '.

Unfortunately Alice was running out of time in the looking-glass world and didn't wait to really enjoy this marvellous poem. Often, when we first come across new poems we feel as Alice did – poetry often sounds good, filling our head with ideas, but because it can be hard to understand *immediately* we rush off too.

What Alice ought to have done (and to some extent she does try to later) was to ask questions, certainly about the words whose meaning she didn't understand. The difficulty she met is that the language the poem is written in is an unfamiliar one. Some of the words are clear English that we understand, but others are total nonsense, in the sense that they cannot be understood.

Lewis Carroll did cheat. He invented some of the words and didn't bother to tell his readers what he intended them all to mean. Yet Alice is absolutely correct. We can at least get the gist of the poem, that somebody killed something, without knowing who or what. What's more, we can also make guesses about what some of these nonsense words mean because they sound like and work in the sentences like words we have heard before:

- 'galumphing' (stanza 5) is obviously meant to be a verb. It looks a bit like gallop and lump and sounds like the noise someone might make as they rode through a wood carrying a heavy weight.

- 'beamish' (stanza 6) seems to be an adjective used to describe the hero. It looks a bit like beaming, which is what people do when they are pleased. So perhaps the word means that the hero has made his father beam with pride.

- 'chortled' (stanza 6) is another verb which seems to be a cross between chuckled and snorted. Carroll invented this word in

1871 when he wrote this poem. It is now an accepted English word, probably because it not only describes a chortle, but actually sounds like one too.

- 'snicker-snack' (stanza 5) is another phrase which sounds like the noise it makes. This has a special name in poetry which we don't really *need* to know ('onomatopoeia', see page 146) in order to comment on how it cleverly imitates the sound of the sword through the flesh of the Jabberwock.

- "Twas' (stanza 1) means 'It was' and this contraction seems old-fashioned to us. Even though the poem was written in the nineteenth century, people didn't talk like that then, so Carroll has deliberately chosen this antiquated form of expression. He wants us to imagine that the poem is a lot older than it really is. There are other examples of obsolete vocabulary too – 'hast' for instance (stanza 6), and the more unusual 'slain' (stanza 6), meaning killed.

- 'Long time the manxome foe he sought' (stanza 3) really means 'he sought (looked for) the manxome foe for a long time'. The syntax is not that of everyday speech and it helps with the pretence that the poem is old. What else does it help with, in terms of the arrangement of words?

- 'The Jabberwock, with eyes of flame' (stanza 4) is an interesting image. We don't know what the beast looks like; in a fantasy world it may well have real fire in its eyes. However, it is more likely that the image here just suggests the frame of mind in which the Jabberwock arrives!

Reading the poem aloud is easy. Although it contains all sorts of strange words and constructions the arrangement of the lines into stanzas, or verses, is very regular. There is a definite beat or rhythm to the lines, and this makes it simple to recite it and to guess which words need stress, which words are important. Likewise, because the poem takes a narrative form (rather like a **ballad**) we feel quite comfortable with what happens. We expect the story to reach a clear (happy?) ending, and so it does. What, though, is the effect of that repeated stanza, of having the first verse again at the end? Is it suggesting that the menace of the Jabberwock might return, and that more of them might inhabit the tulgey wood?

These are the sorts of question Alice might have gone on to ask if only she had time. They are the sorts of question which can be asked about any poem.

James Berry

About the poet

James Berry was born in Jamaica and spent his early life there, moving to Britain in 1948. He has worked as a dental technician and an international telegraphist. Berry always wrote in his spare time and took advantage of redundancy in the 1970s to become a full-time writer. He was soon awarded a Greater London Arts Association Fellowship and spent two days a week as writer in residence at Vauxhall Manor Comprehensive School for a whole year.

While working in the school he realised that schools often have few resources which reflect or celebrate black culture; this encouraged Berry to turn to the promotion of children's books. His first publication, *Bluefoot Traveller* (1976), was an anthology of black writing. Since then he has produced a number of volumes of poetry: *Fractured Circles* (1979), *Lucy's Letters and Loving, Chain of Days* and *When I Dance* (1988). The last of these is a volume of verse written for young people; six of the poems in this volume are taken from it.

James Berry won the National Poetry Prize in 1981. He gives workshops and poetry readings, often with the aim of bringing Caribbean experience to the notice of young people in Britain. In his poems and stories there is a strong sense of the contrast between Inner City Britain and the rural life of the Caribbean. The contrast is made more vivid by Berry's use of both Standard English and Caribbean Nation Language (Creole) with its dancing rhythms, which Berry believes 'widens people's sense of the wholeness of the human family'.

1

What We Said Sitting Making Fantasies

1

I want a talking dog wearing a cap
who can put on gloves
and go to my mum when I'm playing
and she wants a job done.

2

I'd like a great satellite-looking dish
in my garden, drawing together all sounds
of birds' voices, cats' mewing and fighting
crickets' chirping, dogs' barking and fighting
frogs' croaking, guineapigs' squeaking
bicycle-bells ringing, babies' crying
trains' passing, firecrackers' bursts and bangs
into one loud orchestral work
playing once every hour day and night
a new composition every time
so an audience overbrims my garden.

3

At last I have my anger breathalyser
that shows them all –
parents, teachers, friends –
the fires they start
when they make me cross.
I just whip out
my Angerlyser.

Offender watches me blow
hard into it
and sees it swell
its fierce balloon of green
then black then red
and sees it drop and burst
into a flame, three colours
of horned heads and teeth
flaring, jumping, hissing
popping, spluttering –
all round the culprit's feet.
And I just walk away.

4

I'd like a white bull with one horn only
and it's black, and one eyepatch that's black,
and one stripe of red like a bright sash
all around his throat, side and back.
And my bull windowshops from shop to shop
on High Street on his own. And when
my bull moves, his whole red sash flashes
buttons of white lights
advertising my mum's curtains and wallpaper
shop, saying, PICTURES NOT CURTAINS. PETALS
NOT PAPER. FLORAL HOUSE FOR FASHION.

5

My first solo trial flight, you see.
I'm in my flying craft I made myself,
strapped in my seat. Gyrocompass, like
every clockface instrument,
every switch, button and lever, is handy.

In constructing my craft I considered
all problems that affect flying stability.
I considered the aircraft's 'angles of attack'.
I considered its 'lift–drag ratio'.
I considered its 'total reaction'.
Yet when I operate the craft to go
forward, it zooms upward, climbing.
I operate it to descend, it levels
itself, it shoots away forward.
I operate it to climb, my craft spins
round and round and dives
to a perfect touchdown
and settles itself, purring like a cat.
I press a button, I'm unstrapped.
I press a button, I'm flicked up
and out, ejected on to my feet, in front
of the Queen, with her dogs in her garden.
'Hello,' she says. 'You must be Robin Flyer!'
'Yes, mam,' I say. She walks forward.
'Last week, your great-granma was a hundred.'
'Yes, mam. Your telegram came. We celebrated.'
'In her letter of thanks, your gran said
not to be surprised if you dropped
in. And here you are! Well –
stay for tea. Won't you? All
my grandchildren are coming.'
Naturally, I stay for tea, with dogs
and everybody there in the garden.

6

I'd like to have a purple pigeon
who flies up to heaven
and comes back rose-red
flying with trails of pale rainbow ribbons
straight through my window
into my bedroom.

7

I have a three-legged donkey.
I have my three-legged donkey just to see
how he dips his head when he walks
and quickens it up when he gallops.

8

I'd like to see cats with stubby wings
who just before their wings get raised
for a leap on to a bird, they set off
the loudest high pitched siren sound
from the cat's mouth. O, it's a scream
something earsplitting terrible.
Often you see cats losing distance
flying in desperation behind birds
and their on-and-on wailing
scream goes on, cracking up the air.

Pair of Hands against Football

Opposition	You make the cash-tills ring.
Supporters:	You make crowds of people sing.

Goalkeeper's	You make feet jump into a tackle
Supporters:	then make them move into a dribble.
	Football – you draw a million eyes.
	Football – we love your ruses.
	You lead quick feet to strike
	and others to attack the strike
	to outsmart TWO HANDS –
	our GOALKEEPER'S HANDS.

Goalkeeper:	Well, artful ball from the grass,
	you shall not pass
	HANDS like wall
	for you football,
	stopping your triumph-roar
	'cos I'm goalkeeper, you hear –
	HANDS OF TWO
	against eleven heads and feet of
	twenty-two.

Opposition	You make the crowd moan.
Supporters:	You make the crowd go mean.
	You make the crowd leap up aggrieved.
	You make the crowd sit down relieved.

Goalkeeper's	Come on zigzagging like a snake.
Supporters:	You find you have no gate!
	Come on flying like a bird.

See – no cage for a bird!
Come straight like a bullet.
See – you're in HANDS like a wallet!

Goalkeeper: Well, artful ball from the grass,
you shall not pass
HANDS like wall
for you football,
stopping your triumph-roar
'cos I'm goalkeeper, you hear –
HANDS OF TWO
against eleven heads and feet of
    twenty-two.

Opposition   You make the crowd feel relaxed.
Supporters: You make the crowd feel whacked.

Goalkeeper's You make a foot land you on a thigh,
Supporters: make another drive you sky high,
make others turn you into a hare;
you come – our HANDS are there.
You bring a group, close, busy, like lions.
You get knocked up into HANDS of iron.

Goalkeeper: Well, artful ball from the grass,
you shall not pass
HANDS like wall
for you football,
stopping your triumph-roar
'cos I'm goalkeeper, you hear –
HANDS OF TWO
against eleven heads and feet of
    twenty-two.

Goalkeeper's Supporters:	You make us feel washed up but roar at raised winner's cup.
Goalkeeper:	Well, artful ball from the grass, you shall not pass HANDS like wall for you football, stopping your triumph-roar 'cos I'm goalkeeper, you hear – HANDS OF TWO against eleven heads and feet of twenty-two.

Coming of the Sun

The sun came out in England today –
faces cracked wanting to smile.
Overcoats were guests overstayed.
Nakedness wanted to be the rage.

The sun came out echoing on:
people yearned for distant coastlines
and yearned for all good news;
neighbours stood at fences, asking.

The sun came out in England today.
Lambs leapt over each other on hillsides.

Quick Ball Man

for Michael Holding

Bowlerman bowlerman –
O such a wheel-action is quick ball man!

A warrior man
thas such an all-right movement man.

All day him run races,
a-run those poundin riddim paces.

And wicket them a-fly like bullet hit them.
Ball a-hit batsman leg cos it a-fool him.

Batsman a-get caught.
More a-get out fo nought.

More a-come pad-up with runs in them head
but them jus a-come to walk back dead.

And bowlerman is noh jus bowlerman.
The man turn heself now in-a batsman.

And him noh wahn one-one run to get match fix.
Him only wahn six back-a six.

Soh him noh loveless.
Hug-up is regula fram all the mates.

Bowlerman bowlerman –
O such a wheel-action is quick ball man.

Girls Can We Educate We Dads?

Listn the male chauvinist in mi dad –
a girl walkin night street mus be bad.
He dohn sey, the world's a free place
for a girl to keep her unmolested space.
Instead he sey – a girl is a girl.

He sey a girl walkin swingin hips about
call boys to look and shout.
He dohn sey, if a girl have style
she wahn to sey, look
I okay from top to foot.
Instead he sey – a girl is a girl.

Listn the male chauvinist in mi dad –
a girl too laughy-laughy look too glad-glad
jus like a girl too looky-looky roun
will get a pretty satan at her side.
He dohn sey – a girl full of go
dohn wahn stifle talent comin on show.
Instead he sey – a girl is a girl.

Double Act

You laugh keenest because I laugh.
You are upset I feel bad.
We wrestle, jump, fall, play ball.

One bowling, the other batting.
One running, the other timing.
One pinching, the other on watch-keeping.
One eating, the other eating.

Bicycles speed uphill, downhill, on the flat –
we are there, a double act.
You missed our great football day
for me: you too came stiffly dressed
to my sister's wedding.

On birthdays to school we swopped shirts.
Once we tested arm-strength, and the winner
ate a handful of dug-up dirt.

Your last birthday we took turns to make poems.
And you said –
    My mate gobbled up the dinner from the cooker
    and straightaway felt bigger.
    Five of six roast potatoes went down his throat;
    four pounds of beef made him big as a boat.
    Bread pudding and pepsi made him wide;
    he felt like a well packed barrel and sighed.
    My mate could neither go nor come.
    Any wonder his mighty bum?

And I said –
    Shock shock, horror horror!
    I woke up with my mate's monster head:
    my cool, clever one was with him instead.
And you said –
    O, if I fight a bull or climb a mountain
    let me, let me, do it all for Charmaine.
And I said –
    Let me, O let me, be sixteen
    so I catch up with long legged Jean!
And you said –
    I can't, O I can't, stand this love pain
    of a knife cutting through my name!
And I said –
    It's in a man's blood to be weak and feeble
    but it's never on to stand here and dribble.

Out on horse-riding, my horse unsaddled me.
We both came to school with a leg bandaged.

Hurricane

Under low black clouds
the wind was all
speedy feet, all horns and breath,
all bangs, howls, rattles,
in every hen house,
church hall and school.

Roaring, screaming, returning,
it made forced entry, shoved walls,
made rifts, brought roofs down,
hitting rooms to sticks apart.

It wrung soft banana trees,
broke tough trunks of palms.
It pounded vines of yams,
left fields battered up.

Invisible with such ecstasy –
with no intervention of sun or man –
everywhere kept changing branches.

Zinc sheets are kites.
Leaves are panic swarms.
Fowls are fixed with feathers turned.
Goats, dogs, pigs,
all are people together.

Then growling it slunk away
from muddy, mossy trail and boats
in hedges: and cows, ratbats, trees,
fish, all dead in the road.

Haiku Moments

8

New baldheaded glow
again, skyline-face, you start
your old round of climb.

9

Cocks chase gathered hens
village pigs all squeal for feed –
another sunrise.

10

Smells of brewed coffee,
sprats frying up, yams roasted –
soon, church bell for school.

11

Going, dog leads man,
man rides the donkey slowly
leading the white goat.

33

Settled in the bowl
alone banana lies there
cuddle-curved, waiting.

22

Fife-man fife-man O
yu flutin dance in me head –
see, me walk with it!

7

They were white under
stones – downy stems, downy leaves
to be green sunlight.

35

Here along roadside
yellow of gorse announces
sunlight is coming!

Mek Drum Talk, Man

for Caribbean Independence

Budoom-a budoom-a budoom-a ba-dap.
A-dudu-wum a-dudu-wum dudu-wum a-dudu-wum.
Wake skin up. Wake skin.
Slap it up. Slap skin.
Man, slap up drum.
Use yu hundred han them.
Domination get drop.
Some doors get open up.

Lawks O, slap the drum, slap it Buddy.
Slap it like yu a mad mad somody –
budoom-a budoom-a budoom-a ba-dap,
budoom-a budoom-a budoom-a ba-dap.
A-dudu-wum a-dudu-wum dudu-wum a-dudu-wum.
Budoom-a dudu-wum. Budoom-a dudu-wum.
   Bru-dum.

Let out lost ancestor voice.
Let out of skin all pain and vice.
Tell the worl that the king is dead –
forbidden people gettn wed.
Tell towns new words comin fo print –
knowledge looked-fo whe palms they skint.
Get soun like them a talkin gong,
mek them happy jus a-galang

Get the soun, get the soun, get it Buddy.
Wake up gong and family.
Every soun is head with a hum
of deep-deep voice of drum –
tru the windows, tru the trees,
tru the markets, tru the streets.

Lawks O, slap the drum, slap it Buddy.
Slap it like yu a mad mad somody –
budoom-a budoom-a budoom-a ba-dap,
budoom-a budoom-a budoom-a ba-dap.
A-dudu-wum a-dudu-wum dudu-wum a-dudu-wum.
Budoom-a dudu-wum. Budoom-a dudu-wum.
   Bru-dum.

Slap the drum. Elbow drum. Thump drum.
Mek drum sey to be hit is fun.
Wake up skin. Wake up skin
with it broom bu-doom it hidin.
People cry – start a new cycle!
Widen money circle!
Get out every hiddn moan.
Let loose all skin-hiddn groan.

Show off the pulse of big bright sun.
Sen good news to village and town.
Tell the people a child is born,
tell them about a sweet new dawn.
Bring street drummin in the house –
see sleepers get aroused.
Wake the people out-a they trance.
Tell people come dance.

    Lawks O, slap the drum, slap it Buddy.
    Slap it like yu a mad mad somody –
    budoom-a budoom-a budoom-a ba-dap,
    budoom-a budoom-a budoom-a ba-dap.
    A-dudu-wum a-dudu-wum dudu-wum a-dudu-wum.
    Budoom-a dudu-wum. Budoom-a dudu-wum.
      Bru-dum.

Liz Lochhead

About the poet

Liz Lochhead was born in Motherwell, Scotland in 1947. From school she went to Glasgow Art College and then worked as an art teacher. She gave this up to write full time in 1978 when she received the first Scottish/Canadian Writers Exchange Fellowship.

Lochhead's repertoire of writing is diverse. She writes poetry, plays, review sketches, monologues, dialogues, raps, songs and other performance pieces. She also takes part in the performance of her own work. From her Glasgow base she gives readings and workshops throughout the country. She is renowned for her wit and the direct nature of her writing in both Standard English and Scots dialect. Another Scottish poet, Edwin Morgan, described her work in this way:

> Human relationships, especially as seen from a woman's point of view, are central: attraction, pain, acceptance, loss, triumphs and deceptions, habits and surprises; always made immediate through a storyteller's concrete detail of place or voice or object or colour remembered or imagined.

Foreword to *Dreaming Frankenstein*

For Morgan, Lochhead's poetry 'skilled and crafted . . . asks to be read as well as heard'. It can be found in the collections *Memo for Spring* (1972), *The Grimm Sisters* (1981), *Dreaming Frankenstein and Collected Poems* (1984), *True Confessions and New Clichés* (1985) and *Dreaming Bagpipe Muzak* (1991).

What the Creature Said

The blind man did not hate me.
I saw him through the window,
through the rippling circle my own
hot breath had melted
in the spiky flowers of the frost.

I was exhausted,
imagine it. Midwinter. Mountains.
Forest. Dragging my bad leg
over iron ground, impossible passes,
pained by that fleshwound where
that villager's silver bullet
grazed me.

There he was, bent
above the hot soup, supping
his solitude from a bone spoon.
And when my single rap
at the glass spun him full face
towards me, mild as a cat,
my heart stopped but oh
he did not flinch.

Then I saw his
milky eyes stared right through me,
unblinking, and he fumbled
oddly forward to meet me at the latch.
I lifted it and entered,
sure that I found a friend.

The Teachers

they taught
that what you wrote in ink
carried more weight than what you wrote in pencil
and could not be rubbed out.
Punctuation was difficult. Wars
were bad but sometimes necessary
in the face of absolute evil as they knew only too well.
Miss Prentice wore her poppy the whole month of
    November.
Miss Mathieson hit the loud pedal
on the piano and made us sing
The Flowers of the Forest.
Miss Ferguson deplored the Chinese custom
of footbinding but extolled the ingenuity
of terracing the paddyfields.
Someone she'd once known had given her a kimono
    and a parasol.
Miss Prentice said the Empire had enlightened people
and been a two way thing.
The Dutch grew bulbs and were our allies in
wooden shoes.

We grew bulbs on the window sills
beside the frogspawn that quickened into wriggling
commas or stayed full stop.
Some people in our class were stupid, full stop.
The leather tawse was coiled around the sweetie tin
in her desk beside the box of coloured blackboard chalk
Miss Ferguson never used.

Miss Prentice wore utility smocks.
Miss Mathieson had a moustache.
If your four-needled knitting got no
further than the heel you couldn't turn
then she'd keep you at your helio sewing
till its wobbling cross-stitch was specked with rusty
   blood.

Spelling hard words was easy when you knew how.

Man on a Bench

This old man
has grown year-weary
no joy in changing seasons, just
another blooming spring
another sodden summer
another corny old autumn
and another winter
to leave him cold.

The Choosing

We were first equal Mary and I
with same coloured ribbons in mouse-coloured hair
and with equal shyness,
we curtseyed to the lady councillor
for copies of Collins' Children's Classics.
First equal, equally proud.

Best friends too Mary and I
a common bond in being cleverest (equal)
in our small school's small class.
I remember
the competition for top desk
or to read aloud the lesson
at school service.
And my terrible fear
of her superiority at sums.

I remember the housing scheme
where we both stayed.
The same houses, different homes,
where the choices got made.

I don't know exactly why they moved,
but anyway they went.
Something about a three-apartment
and a cheaper rent.
But from the top deck of the high-school bus
I'd glimpse among the others on the corncr
Mary's father, mufflered, contrasting strangely
with the elegant greyhounds by his side.

He didn't believe in high school education,
especially for girls,
or in forking out for uniforms.

Ten years later on a Saturday –
I am coming from the library –
sitting near me on the bus,
Mary
with a husband who is tall,
curly haired, has eyes
for no one else but Mary.

Her arms are round the full-shaped vase
that is her body.
Oh, you can see where the attraction lies
in Mary's life –
not that I envy her, really.

And I am coming from the library
with my arms full of books.
I think of those prizes that were ours for the taking
and wonder when the choices got made
we don't remember making.

Poem for My Sister

My little sister likes to try my shoes,
to strut in them,
admire her spindle-thin twelve-year-old legs
in this season's styles.
She says they fit perfectly,
but wobbles
on their high heels, they're
hard to balance.

I like to watch my little sister
playing hopscotch, admire the
    neat hops-and-skips of her,
their quick peck,
never-missing their mark, not
over-stepping the line.
She is competent at peever.

I try to warn my little sister
about unsuitable shoes,
point out my own distorted feet, the callouses,
odd patches of hard skin.
I should not like to see her
in my shoes.
I wish she would stay
sure footed,
                    sensibly shod.

Grandfather's Room

In your room in the clutter of pattern
you lie.
Sunlight strains through lace curtains,
makes shadow patterns
on wallpaper's faded trellises,
on fat paisley cushions,
on the gingham table-cloth.
On the carpet, rugs
layer on layer like the years,
pattern on pattern,
cover the barest patches.
Geometric, floral, hand-made rag rugs,
an odd bit left over from the neighbours'
new stair carpet –
patterns all familiar
from other people's houses,
other people's lives.

In a clutter of patterns
you lie,
your shrunken head, frail
as a shell or a bird skull,
peeps from the crazy-paved
patch-work quilt.

Above your bed
in his framed death,your son,
my Uncle Robert that I never knew.

They say
he was well-known for his singing at weddings
and was a real nice lad, killed
in the war at twenty-one.
His photo, hung so long in the same place has
merged with the wallpaper,
faded into the pattern.
(But it can't be moved now,
it has left its mark.)
Uncle Robert in a uniform
above your bedside table-top, the
medicines, the bright and bullet-shaped pills,
nothing in the angle of his smile
nor in the precise tilt of his cap, hinting
how soon, how suddenly he was to die.

There he is in black and white, believable.
Oh yes, he smiled and sang.
His sudden death stopped short
a slower certain dying, change.
While the other wall holds up
a scrap of nineteen thirty three,
maintains its true.
A photo of the family (or so they say)
that flop-haired boy my balding father?
and you, grandfather, tall and strong,
smouldering in a landscape of shut pits and
     silent chimneys?
It's framed like a fact,
set fair and square but has less weight
is less real
than those faint patterns traced
by a weak sun through lace curtains.
Pale shadows, constantly changing.

For My Grandmother Knitting

There is no need they say
but the needles still move
their rhythms in the working of your hands
as easily
as if your hands
were once again those sure and skilful hands
of the fisher-girl.

You are old now
and your grasp of things is not so good
but master of your movements then
deft and swift
you slit the still-ticking quick silver fish.
Hard work it was too
of necessity.

But now they say there is no need
as the needles move
in the working of your hands
once the hands of the bride
with the hand-span waist
once the hands of the miner's wife
who scrubbed his back
in a tin bath by the coal fire
once the hands of the mother
of six who made do and mended
scraped and slaved slapped sometimes
when necessary.

But now they say there is no need
the kids they say grandma
have too much already
more than they can wear
too many scarves and cardigans –
gran you do too much
there's no necessity.

At your window you wave
them goodbye Sunday.
With your painful hands
big on shrunken wrists.
Swollen-jointed. Red. Arthritic. Old.
But the needles still move
their rhythms in the working of your hands
easily
as if your hands remembered
of their own accord the pattern
as if your hands had forgotten
how to stop.

Poppies

My father said she'd be fined
at best, jailed maybe, the lady
whose high heels shattered the silence.
I sat on his knee, we were listening
to the silence on the radio.
My mother tutted, oh that it was terrible,
as over our air
those sharp heeltaps struck steel, rang clear
as a burst of gunfire or a laugh
through those wired-up silent streets around the
    Cenotaph.
Respect.
Remembrance.
Surely when all was said
two minutes silence in November
wasn't much to ask for, for the dead?
Poppies on the mantelpiece, the photograph
of a boy in a forage cap, the polished
walnut veneer of the wireless,
the buzzing in the ears and when
the silence ended the heldfire voice
of the commentator, who was shocked,
naturally, but not
wanting to make too much of it.
Why did she do it?
Was she taken sick – but that was no
excuse, on the radio it said,
couldn't you picture it?
how grown soldiers buttoned in their uniforms
keeled over, fell like flies
trying to keep up the silence.

Maybe it was looking at the khaki button eye
and the woundwire stem
of the redrag poppy
pinned in her proper lapel
that made the lady stick a bloody bunch of them
behind her ear
and clash those high heels across the square,
a dancer.

Riddle-Me-Ree

My first is in life (not contained within heart)
My second's in whole but never in part.
My third's in forever, but also in vain.
My last's in ending, why not in pain?

is love the answer?

Wedding March

Could I buy a white dress and hope for good weather?
Could I take something borrowed? Could we bind us
    together?
And while Visions of Sugar Plums danced in each head,
Could we lie long content on the bed that we'd made?

No, I've not my own house in order enough
To ever make you a tidy wife.
Could I learn to waste not
And want not –
Make soup from bones,
Save wool scraps, bake scones
From sour milk. Would I ask for more
Than to lunch alone on what's left over from the night
    before.
Could I soothe our children's night time bad dream fear
With nursery rhymes, and never find my cupboard bare?
Imagine an old handbag full of photographs.
Once in a blue moon I'd drag them out for laughs –
Smiling at poses I once carefully arranged,
In hoots at the hemlines and how we've changed.

We'll try. It still is early days.
I'll try and mend my sluttish ways.
We'll give our kitchen a new look –
A lick of paint, a spice rack, and a recipe book.
I'll watch our tangled undies bleaching clean
In the humdrum of the laundromat machine.
I'll take my pet dog vacuum on its daily walk through
    rooms.
And knowing there is no clean sweep,
keep busy still with brooms.

I Wouldn't Thank You for a Valentine

(Rap)

I wouldn't thank you for a Valentine.
I won't wake up early wondering if the postman's been.
Should 10 red-padded satin hearts arrive with sticky
    sickly saccharine
Sentiments in very vulgar verses I wouldn't wonder if
    you meant them.
Two dozen anonymous Interflora roses?
I'd not bother to swither over who sent them!
I wouldn't thank you for a Valentine.

Scrawl SWALK across the envelope
I'd just say 'Same Auld Story
I canny be bothered deciphering it –
I'm up to hear with Amore!
The whole Valentine's Day Thing is trivial and
    commercial,
A cue for unleashing cliches and candyheart motifs to
    which I personally am not partial.'
Take more than singing Telegrams, or pints of
    Chanel Five, or sweets,
To get me ordering oysters or ironing my black satin
    sheets.
I wouldn't thank you for a Valentine.

If you sent me a solitaire and promises solemn,
Took out an ad in the Guardian Personal Column
Saying something very soppy such as 'Who Loves Ya,
   Poo?
I'll tell you, I do, Fozzy Bear, that's who!'
You'd entirely fail to charm me, in fact I'd detest it
I wouldn't be eighteen again for anything, I'm glad I'm
   past it.
I wouldn't thank you for a Valentine.

If you sent me a single orchid, or a pair of Janet Reger's
   in a heartshaped box and declared your Love Eternal
I'd say I'd not be caught dead in them they were
   politically suspect and I'd rather something thermal.
If you hired a plane and blazed our love in a banner
   across the skies;
If you bought me something flimsy in a flatteringly
   wrong size;
If you sent me a postcard with three Xs and told me
   how you felt
I wouldn't thank you, I'd melt.

Favourite Shade

(Rap)

She's getting No More Black, her.
You've got bugger all bar black, Barbra.
Black's dead drab an' all.
Ah'd never have been seen
deid in it, your age tae!
Dreich. As a shade it's draining.
Better aff
somethin tae pit a bit a colour in her cheeks, eh no?

Black. Hale wardrobe fulla black claes.
Jist hingin' therr half the time, emmty.
On the hangers, hingin.
Plus by the way a gloryhole
Chockablock with bermuda shorts, the lot.
Yella kimono, ah don't know
whit all.
Tropical prints.
Polyester everything Easy-Kerr. Bit naw, naw
that was last year, noo
she's no one to give
nothing coloured
houseroom. Black. Black.
Ah'm fed up tae the back teeth lukkin' ett her.
Feyther says the same.

Who's peyin' fur it onlywey?
Wance yir workin' weer whit yi like.
No as if yiv nothin' tae pit oan yir back.
Black!
As well oot the world as oot the fashion.

Seen a wee skirt in Miss Selfridge.
Sort of dove, it was lovely.
Would she weer it, but?
Goes: see if it was black
If it was black
it'd be brilliant.

Charles Causley

About the poet

Charles Causley was born in
the town of Launceston,
Cornwall in 1917 and, apart
from a time spent serving in the
Royal Navy during World War
II, he has lived his whole life in
that county. Cornwall is rich in
wild geography, local legend, history, gossip and mystery,
elements which Causley weaves into all his work, reflecting the love
of his home. 'Poetry, however unlikely its subject, theme or surface
appearance, has always been to me a particular form of autobiography,' wrote Causley in the notes to his *Collected Poems: 1951–75*.
The influence of traditional ballad and song is evident in his narrative
poems and lyrics, and his sense of humour is strong, not least in the
poetry that he writes for children.

As deputy head of a primary school in Launceston for many years, it
is natural that Causley should have an interest in poetry for young
children. He has edited anthologies of verse for them including
The Puffin Book of Magic Verse and written for them himself in his
collections *Figgie Hobbin* (1970) and *Jack the Treacle Eater* (1987).
His poetry for adults can be found in *Farewell, Aggie Weston* (1951),
Survivor's Leave (1953), *Union Street* (1957), *Johnny Alleluia* (1961)
and *Underneath the Water* (1968).

A Fellow of the Royal Society of Literature, Causley has been
awarded the Queen's Gold Medal for Poetry (1967), the Signal
Poetry Award (1986) and the Ingersoll/T.S. Eliot Award (1990). He
received the CBE in 1986.

What Has Happened to Lulu?

What has happened to Lulu, mother?
    What has happened to Lu?
There's nothing in her bed but an old rag doll
    And by its side a shoe.

Why is her window wide, mother,
    The curtain flapping free,
And only a circle on the dusty shelf
    Where her money-box used to be?

Why do you turn your head, mother,
    And why do the tear-drops fall?
And why do you crumple that note on the fire
    And say it is nothing at all?

I woke to voices late last night,
    I heard an engine roar.
Why do you tell me the things I heard
    Were a dream and nothing more?

I heard somebody cry, mother,
    In anger or in pain,
But now I ask you why, mother,
    You say it was a gust of rain.

Why do you wander about as though
    You don't know what to do?
What has happened to Lulu, mother?
    What has happened to Lu?

The Ballad of Charlotte Dymond

Charlotte Dymond, a domestic servant aged eighteen, was
murdered near Rowtor Ford on Bodmin Moor on Sunday
14 April 1844 by her young man: a crippled farm-hand,
Matthew Weeks, aged twenty-two. A stone marks the spot.

It was a Sunday evening
   And in the April rain
That Charlotte went from our house
   And never came home again.

Her shawl of diamond redcloth,
   She wore a yellow gown,
She carried the green gauze handkerchief
   She bought in Bodmin town.

About her throat her necklace
   And in her purse her pay:
The four silver shillings
   She had at Lady Day.

In her purse four shillings
   And in her purse her pride
As she walked out one evening
   Her lover at her side.

Out beyond the marshes
   Where the cattle stand,
With her crippled lover
   Limping at her hand.

Charlotte walked with Matthew
  Through the Sunday mist,
Never saw the razor
  Waiting at his wrist.

Charlotte she was gentle
  But they found her in the flood
Her Sunday beads among the reeds
  Beaming with her blood.

Hayley
Amy
Frances

Matthew, where is Charlotte,
  And wherefore has she flown?
For you walked out together
  And now are come alone.

Why do you not answer,
  Stand silent as a tree,
Your Sunday worsted stockings
  All muddied to the knee?

Why do you mend your breast-pleat
  With a rusty needle's thread
And fall with fears and silent tears
  Upon your single bed?

Why do you sit so sadly
  Your face the colour of clay
And with a green gauze handkerchief
  Wipe the sour sweat away?

Has she gone to Blisland
   To seek an easier place,
And is that why your eye won't dry
   And blinds your bleaching face?

Take me home!' cried Charlotte,
   'I lie here in the pit!
A red rock rests upon my breasts
   And my naked neck is split!'

Her skin was soft as sable,
   Her eyes were wide as day,
Her hair was blacker than the bog
   That licked her life away.

Her cheeks were made of honey,
   Her throat was made of flame
Where all around the razor
   Had written its red name.

As Matthew turned at Plymouth
   About the tilting Hoe,
The cold and cunning constable
   Up to him did go:

'I've come to take you, Matthew,
   Unto the magistrate's door.
Come quiet now, you pretty poor boy,
   And you must know what for.'

'She is as pure,' cried Matthew,
    'As is the early dew,
Her only stain it is the pain
    That round her neck I drew!

'She is as guiltless as the day
    She sprang forth from her mother.
The only sin upon her skin
    Is that she loved another.'

They took him off to Bodmin,
    They pulled the prison bell,
They sent him smartly up to heaven
    And dropped him down to hell.

All through the granite kingdom
    And on its travelling airs
Ask which of these two lovers
    The most deserves your prayers.

And your steel heart search, Stranger,
    That you may pause and pray
For lovers who come not to bed
    Upon their wedding day,

But lie upon the moorland
    Where stands the sacred snow
Above the breathing river,
    And the salt sea-winds go.

Everyone

Young Edgcumbe

Young Edgcumbe spoke by the river,
  Young Edgcumbe spoke by the sea,
'The King with the crown in London town
  Shall never be King to me.

'For he has taken the old King's son
  That is both young and fair,
And wound a prison pillow round
  His head and yellow hair.

'And then he took the other
  That by his brother lay
And with a pin his royal skin
  Of breath has pricked away.

'O never shall young Edgcumbe
  Bow or bend the knee
Or speak or sing "Long live the King"
  To such a man as he.'

But when to London water
  Young Edgcumbe's words were sped,
'He is alive,' the cold King cried,
  'But is already dead!'

Down by the Tamar river
  As young Edgcumbe walked by,
He heard from sleep the woodcock leap
  Into the sudden sky.

As under Cotehele tower
    Young Edgcumbe listening stood,
A branch that broke to Edgcumbe spoke
    Of strangers in the wood.

All under Cotehele tower
    He heard Bodrugan shout,
'Young Edgcumbe yield, for sword and shield
    Ring your good land about!'

But young Edgcumbe was bonny,
    His wits bright as a brand,
And pass and ride on Cotehele side
    He knew as his right hand.

In scarlet-red the sentry
    By the wood-gate did lie,
But redder far the shirt he wore
    When young Edgcumbe passed by.

The King's man for young Edgcumbe
    Lay cold under the hill,
Till Edgcumbe's knife searched out his life
    And left him colder still.

Young Edgcumbe walked by the water,
    Young Edgcumbe walked by the shore,
Bodrugan's steel was at his heel
    And the spring flood before.

Young Edgcumbe took his bonnet
    As he stood on the steep,
And with a stone his cap has thrown
    Into the waters deep.

Light was young Edgcumbe's bonnet,
    Heavy the stone he spun
That struck the swell clear as the bell
    Of Cotehele calling one.

'Alas for poor young Edgcumbe!'
    He heard Bodrugan say.
'For no man from that flood may come
    To fight another day.

'See on the running river
    His cap swims like a snow.
And white as milk, in watered silk
    Young Edgcumbe lies below.

'Farewell, farewell young Edgcumbe,'
    He heard Bodrugan call.
'The river loud it is your shroud
    And the pure sky your pall.

'And now to royal London
    From the far Cornish shore
This message bring unto the King:
    Young Edgcumbe is no more.'

But close as his ten fingers
    And close as hip and thigh,
Young Edgcumbe sees through forest trees
    Bodrugan pass him by.

And when came on the evening
    Young Edgcumbe sailed the Sound,
Nor laid his head on prison bed,
    Nor trod the prison ground.

O when came on the evening
   Young Edgcumbe sailed the sea,
And in the rare and morning air
   Has come to Brittany.

And with bold Henry Tudor
   Young Edgcumbe spoke as friend,
And freely swore in peace and war
   To serve him to life's end.

Now on the tide to England
   Young Edgcumbe's home again
Where King and crown are both cast down
   On bloody Bosworth plain.

And at the scarlet feast of war
   Men drank the bitter cup,
And one King lay as cold as clay,
   And one there was stood up.

Before the throne of England
   Young Edgcumbe now does stand,
Swears on the ring of England's King
   And kisses his gold hand.

'Young Edgcumbe, Lord of Cotehele,
   Bodrugan's Lord shall be,
His house and land yours to command
   Beside the Cornish sea!'

Across the Bodmin moorland
   Young Edgcumbe's horsemen drum.
Bodrugan fears, Bodrugan hears
   The sounding hoof-beats come.

'I ride,' then cried young Edgcumbe,
   'As once you rode for me.
Whom you would slay and was the prey
   The hunter now shall be.'

He rode him down the valley,
   He rode him up the steep,
Till white as wood Bodrugan stood
   Above the Cornish deep.

And from the height, Bodrugan
   Sprang down into the swell
That tide on tide at the cliff-side
   Hammers a passing-bell.

And ever did the ocean
   Under Bodrugan's Leap
With loving care the body fair
   Of Lord Bodrugan keep.

And when again to Cotehele
   Young Edgcumbe he did ride,
A house of prayer he builded there
   Above the water-side.

And still by Cotehele manor
   The river-chapel stands,
And at Bodrugan's Leap the deep
   Still wrings its watery hands,

Though Edgcumbe and Bodrugan
   Long, long they sleep, and sound:
The one his grave in the green wave,
   The other in green ground.

My Mother Saw a Dancing Bear

My mother saw a dancing bear
By the schoolyard, a day in June.
The keeper stood with chain and bar
And whistle-pipe, and played a tune.

And bruin lifted up its head
And lifted up its dusty feet,
And all the children laughed to see
It caper in the summer heat.

They watched as for the Queen it died.
They watched it march. They watched it halt.
They heard the keeper as he cried,
'Now, roly-poly!' 'Somersault!'

And then, my mother said, there came
The keeper with a begging-cup,
The bear with burning coat of fur,
Shaming the laughter to a stop.

They paid a penny for the dance,
But what they saw was not the show;
Only, in bruin's aching eyes,
Far-distant forests, and the snow.

I Saw a Jolly Hunter

I saw a jolly hunter
   With a jolly gun
Walking in the country
   In the jolly sun.

In the jolly meadow
   Sat a jolly hare.
Saw the jolly hunter.
   Took jolly care.

Hunter jolly eager –
   Sight of jolly prey.
Forgot gun pointing
   Wrong jolly way.

Jolly hunter jolly head
   Over heels gone.
Jolly old safety catch
   Not jolly on.

Bang went the jolly gun.
   Hunter jolly dead.
Jolly hare got clean away.
   Jolly good, I said.

Richard Bartlett

Reading the ninety-year-old paper singed
By time, I meet my shadowed grandfather,
Richard Bartlett, stone-cutter, quarryman;
The Bible Christian local preacher, Sunday
School teacher and teetotaller. *Highly
Respected, leading and intelligent
Member of the sect. He will be greatly missed.
Leaves wife and family of seven children,
The youngest being three months old.*

Nine on a July morning: Richard Bartlett
About to split a stone, trying to find
A place to insert the wedge. The overhang
Shrugs off a quiet sting of slate. It nags
Three inches through the skull. Richard Bartlett
Never spoke after he was struck. Instead
Of words the blood and brains kept coming.
They lugged him in a cart to the Dispensary.
Never a chance of life, the doctors said.
He lived until twelve noon. His mate, Melhuish,
Searched for, but never found, the killing stone.
The fees of the jury were given to the widow.

The funeral was a thunder of hymns and prayers.
Two ministers, churchyard a checkerboard
Pieced with huge black: the family nudged nearer
The pit where the Workhouse was, and a leper's life
On the Parish. And in my grandmother
Was lit a sober dip of fear, unresting
Till her death in the year of the Revolution:
Her children safely fled like beads of mercury
Over the scattered map. I close the paper,
Its print of mild milk-chocolate. Bend to the poem,
Trying to find a place to insert the wedge.

Dick Lander

When we were children at the National School
We passed each day, clipped to the corner of
Old Sion Street, Dick Lander, six foot four,
Playing a game of trains with match-boxes.

He poked them with a silver-headed cane
In the seven kinds of daily weather God
Granted the Cornish. Wore a rusted suit.
It dangled off him like he was a tree.

My friend Sid Bull, six months my senior, and
A world authority on medicine,
Explained to me just what was wrong with Dick.
'Shell-shopped,' he said. 'You catch it in the war.'

We never went too close to Dick in case
It spread like measles. 'Shell-shopped, ain't you, Dick?'
The brass-voiced Sid would bawl. Dick never spoke.
Carried on shunting as if we weren't there.

My Auntie said before he went away
Dick was a master cricketer. Could run
As fast as light. Was the town joker. Had
Every girl after him. Was spoiled quite out

Of recognition, and at twenty-one
Looked set to take the family business on
(Builders' merchants, seed, wool, manure and corn).
'He's never done a day's work since they sent

'Him home after the Somme,' my Uncle grinned.
'If he's mazed as a brush, my name's Lord George.
Why worry if the money's coming in?'
At firework time we throw a few at Dick.

Shout, 'Here comes Kaiser Bill!' Dick stares us through
As if we're glass. We yell, 'What did you do
In the Great War?' And skid into the dark.
'Choo, choo,' says Dick. 'Choo, choo, choo, choo, choo,
    choo.'

Six Women

Six women in a chronic ward, the light
Like dirty water filtering away;
Washed, spruced, and fed, they innocently wear
Their flowered shrouds to face the last of day.

One, flapping endlessly, a landed fish,
Thumps on a beach of sheets. One lies and glares
At her reflection in the ceiling's paint,
Writhes to avoid its gaze, and gabbles prayers.

One, deaf as granite, smiles, begins to speak
To someone she, and she alone, has spied;
Calls from the deep and dewy field her cat,
Holds it, invisible, at her clenched side.

One, crouching, poised as if to pounce, stone-still,
Suddenly gives a start, a little squeak:
A mouse-woman with wild and whitened hair,
Dried flakes of tears like snow cooling her cheek.

One, bird-like, lifting up her blinded head
To sounds beyond the television-blare
Cries out, in a sharp sliver of a voice,
I do not know if anyone is there!

I do not know if anyone is here.
If so, if not so, I must let it be.
I hold your drifted hand; no time to tell
What six dead women hear, or whom they see.

Ward 14

Today, incredibly, the nurse
Attempts to reason with her –
The mother with the brain three quarters struck away

By apoplexy, and other
Assorted fevers and indignities as the body
Slides slowly, O so slowly, to harbour.

'Wake up!' orders the nurse, kindly.
'Open your eyes.'

The mother does so.
'Your son is here,' says the nurse:
A razor-voice stained momentarily with a little sugar.

'You mustn't cry
When your son is here.
Mothers don't cry
When their sons are here.
Now be a good girl;
That's a good girl.'

Puzzled, the mother stares at her:
Wonder creasing the face.
'You're going to be a good girl
Now that your son is here
Aren't you?'
'Yes,' says the mother rapidly,
Wide-eyed, astounded.

Her task accomplished, the nurse
Clops purposefully away down the ward
Like a fractious charger
After a small battle.

As soon as she has gone, the mother
Breaks once more into swift, unceasing tears
Of pain, misery, frustration.
The other visitors look at the son
With a compassionate air;
Rather less so at the patient.

Weep on, mother!
It is your right.
It is your due.
Helpless at the foot of your crucifixion
He is not going to deny you that.

Scenes of Childhood

IV Stang Hunt

Waking, aged four, I heard under the steep
Window a hunting horn, a scat of tin
Trays, kitchen pans, sycamore whistles, hob-
Nails punishing the hill. In my nightshirt

I ran to where my mother, father drew
An inch of curtain back, the oil lamp thinned
To a wafer of light, half gold, half winking blue.
I caught a blare of torches. The rough song.

'Stang hunt. It means a man was wicked to
His family,' was what my father said.
Beneath my naked feet, unseen, unknown,
Trembled the first small shock of ice, of stone.

School at Four O'Clock

At four o'clock the building enters harbour.
All day it seems that we have been at sea.
Now, having lurched through the last of the water,
We lie, stone-safe, beside the jumping quay.
The stiff waves propped against the classroom window,
The razor-back of cliffs we never pass,
The question-mark of green coiling behind us,
Have all turned into cabbages, slates, grass.

Up the slow hill a squabble of children wanders
As silence dries the valley like a drought,
When suddenly that speechless cry is raging
Once more round these four walls to be let out.
Like playing cards the Delabole slates flutter,
The founding stone is shaken in its mine,
The faultless evening light begins to stutter
As the cry hurtles down the chimney-spine.

Packing my bag with useless bits of paper
I wonder, when the last word has been said,
If I'd prefer to find each sound was thudding
Not round the school, but just inside my head.
I watch where the street lamp with sodium finger
Touches the darkening voices as they fall.
Outside? Inside? Perhaps either condition's
Better than his who hears nothing at all.

And I recall another voice. A teacher
Long years ago, saying, *I think I know*
Where all the children come from, but the puzzle
To me is, as they grow up, where they go?
Love, wonder, marvellous hope. All these can wither
With crawling years like flowers on a stalk;
Or, to some Piper's tune, vanish for ever
As creatures murdered on a morning walk.

Though men may blow this building up with powder,
Drag its stone guts to knacker's yard, or tip,
Smash its huge heart to dust, and spread the shingle
By the strong sea, or sink it like a ship –
Listen. Through the clear shell of air the voices
Still strike like water from the mountain bed;
The cry of those who to a certain valley
Hungry and innocent came. And were not fed.

I Am the Song

I am the song that sings the bird.
I am the leaf that grows the land.
I am the tide that moves the moon.
I am the stream that halts the sand.
I am the cloud that drives the storm.
I am the earth that lights the sun.
I am the fire that strikes the stone.
I am the clay that shapes the hand.
I am the word that speaks the man.

Grace Nichols

About the poet

Grace Nichols was born in Georgetown, Guyana in 1950. She spent her youth and early adulthood in the Caribbean and the colour and light of her childhood emerge in the vitality of her poetry. She worked as a freelance reporter and journalist, moving to Britain in 1977. She lives in Lewes, Sussex and has a daughter, Lesley, who also writes.

Grace Nichols is a poet and novelist who also collects and edits anthologies of poetry for young people. She is also a professional speaker and performer. She won the Commonwealth Poetry Prize in 1983 and her published poetry collections, written in Standard English and Caribbean Nation Language, are *i is a long-memoried woman* (1983), *The Fat Black Woman's Poems* (1984) and *Lazy Thoughts of a Lazy Woman* (1989).

Iguana Memory

Saw an iguana once
when I was very small
in our backdam backyard
came rustling across my path

green like moving newleaf sunlight

big like big big lizard
with more legs than centipede
so it seemed to me
and it must have stopped a while
eyes meeting mine
iguana and child locked in a brief
split moment happening
before it went hurrying

       for the green of its life

Be a Butterfly

Don't be a kyatta-pilla
Be a butterfly
old preacher screamed
to illustrate his sermon
of Jesus and the higher life

rivulets of well-earned
sweat sliding down
his muscly mahogany face
in the half-empty school church
we sat shaking with muffling
laughter
watching our mother trying to save
herself from joining the wave

only our father remaining poker face
and afterwards we always went home to
split peas Sunday soup
with dumplings, fufu and pigtail

Don't be a kyatta-pilla
Be a butterfly
Be a butterfly

That was de life preacher
and you was right

The Fat Black Woman Goes Shopping

Shopping in London winter
is a real drag for the fat black woman
going from store to store
in search of accommodating clothes
and de weather so cold

Look at the frozen thin mannequins
fixing her with grin
and de pretty face salesgals
exchanging slimming glances
thinking she don't notice

Lord is aggravating

Nothing soft and bright and billowing
to flow like breezy sunlight
when she walking

The fat black woman curses in Swahili/Yoruba
and nation language under her breathing
all this journeying and journeying

The fat black woman could only conclude
that when it came to fashion
the choice is lean

    Nothing much beyond size 14

Beauty

Beauty
is a fat black woman
walking the fields
pressing a breezed
hibiscus
to her cheek
while the sun lights up
her feet

Beauty
is a fat black woman
riding the waves
drifting in happy oblivion
while the sea turns back
to hug her shape

Spring

After two unpredictable spells
of influenza that winter
I was taking no chances
(not even to put the rubbish outside)

pulling on my old black jacket
resolutely winding
a scarf round and round my neck
winter rituals I had grown to
accept
with all the courage of an unemerged
butterfly
I unbolted the door and stepped outside

only to have that daffodil baby
kick me in the eye

Abra-Cadabra

My mother had more magic
in her thumb
than the length and breadth
of any magician

Weaving incredible stories
around the dark-green senna brew
just to make us slake
the ritual Sunday purgative

Knowing when to place a cochineal poultice
on a fevered forehead
Knowing how to measure a belly's symmetry
kneading the narah pains away

Once my baby sister stuffed
a split-pea up her nostril
my mother got a crochet needle
and gently tried to pry it out

We stood around her
like inquisitive gauldings

Suddenly, in surgeon's tone she ordered,
'Pass the black pepper,'
and patted a little
under the dozing nose

My baby sister sneezed.
The rest was history.

Wha Me Mudder Do

Mek me tell you wha me Mudder do
wha me mudder do
wha me mudder do

Me mudder pound plantain mek fufu
Me mudder catch crab mek calaloo stew

Mek me tell you wha me mudder do
wha me mudder do
wha me mudder do

Me mudder beat hammer
Me mudder turn screw
she paint chair red
then she paint it blue

Mek me tell you wha me mudder do
wha me mudder do
wha me mudder do

Me mudder chase bad-cow
with one 'Shoo'
she paddle down river
in she own canoe
Ain't have nothing
dat me mudder can't do
Ain't have nothing
dat me mudder can't do

Mek me tell you

Praise Song for My Mother

You were
water to me
deep and bold and fathoming

You were
moon's eye to me
pull and grained and mantling

You were
sunrise to me
rise and warm and streaming

You were
the fishes red gill to me
the flame tree's spread to me
the crab's leg/the fried plantain smell
                              replenishing replenishing

Go to your wide futures, you said

On Her Way to Recovery

My thirteen-year-old daughter
is now taller than me.
Illness seemed to have stretched her a bit.

She, who was on her back
for four days and four nights,
feverish, heavy limbed, uneating,

Got up this morning
pulled on her sneakers, my long red dressing gown,
and went out into the garden.

'Don't worry,' she says,
coming suddenly into the room
where I'm lying, 'I dressed warm.'

Startled. Pleased.
I glance up at the red-robed gazelle
on her way to recovery.

Hey There Now!

for Lesley

Hey there now
my brownwater flower
      my sunchild branching
from my mountain river
      hey there now!
my young stream
         headlong
            rushing
I love to watch you
      when you're
         sleeping
            blushing

Conkers

Autumn treasures
from the horsechestnut tree

Lying roly poly
among their split green casings

Shiny and hard
like pops of polished mahogany

An English schoolboy
picking them up –

The same compulsive
fickle avidity –

As I picked up
orange-coloured cockles

Way back then
from a tropical childhood tree

Hand about to close in . . .
then spotting another even better

Now, waiting on our bus
we grown-ups watch him

Not knowing how or why
we've lost our instinct

For gathering
the magic shed of trees

Though in partyful mood
in wineful spirits

We dance around crying,
'Give me back my conker.'

Two Old Black Men on a Leicester Square Park Bench

What do you dream of you
old black men sitting
on park benches staunchly
wrapped up in scarves
and coats of silence
eyes far away from the cold
grey and strutting
pigeon
ashy fingers trembling
(though it's said that the old
hardly ever feel the cold)

do you dream revolutions
you could have forged
or mourn
some sunfull woman you
might have known a
hibiscus flower
ghost memories of desire

O it's easy
to rainbow the past
after all the letters from
home spoke of hardships

and the sun was traded long ago

On Receiving a Jamaican Postcard

Colourful native entertainers
dancing at de edge of de sea
a man-an-woman combination
choreographing
de dream of de tourist industry

de two a dem in smiling conspiracy
to capture dis dream of de tourist industry

an de sea blue
an de sky blue
an de sand gold fuh true

an de sea blue
an de sky blue
an de sand gold fuh true

He staging a dance-prance
head in a red band
beating he waist drum
as if he want to drown she wid sound
an yes, he muscle looking strong

She a vision of frilly red
back-backing to he riddum
exposing she brown leg
arcing like lil mo
she will limbo into de sea

Anything fuh de sake of de tourist industry
Anything fuh de sake of de tourist industry

John Betjeman

About the poet

John Betjeman was born in Highgate, London in 1906. From school at Marlborough College, Wiltshire, he went to Magdalen College, Oxford. Betjeman enjoyed his youth and eventually immortalised it in his blank verse autobiography **Summoned by Bells** (published much later, in 1960). However, the enjoyment got in the way of his studies and Betjeman left Oxford without a degree to become the cricket master in a preparatory school.

Betjeman's interests were wide and before long he had become the film critic of the London **Evening Standard**. He was later to write for the **Architectural Review** and became the general editor of the **Shell Guides to Britain** series in 1934. His poetry appeared in many volumes, from **Mount Zion** (1931), his first collection of verse, to later and more well-known volumes: **New Bats in Old Belfries** (1945), **A Few Late Chrysanthemums** (1954), **A Nip in the Air** (1972) and **High and Low** (1976).

In 1972, on the death of Cecil Day Lewis, Betjeman was created Poet Laureate, remaining so until his own death in 1984. He was eminently suited to this honour: his cheerful, gently ironic poetry looks back at an England which he felt was fast disappearing under the ravages of modern town planning. His tone is light-heartedly English, yet, beneath the jollity, Sir John Betjeman was a serious and often melancholy poet.

Dilton Marsh Halt

Was it worth keeping the Halt open,
  We thought as we looked at the sky
Red through the spread of the cedar-tree,
  With the evening train gone by?

Yes, we said, for in summer the anglers use it,
  Two and sometimes three
Will bring their catches of rods and poles and perches
  To Westbury, home to tea.

There isn't a porter. The platform is made of sleepers.
  The guard of the last up-train puts out the light
And high over lorries and cattle the Halt unwinking
  Waits through the Wiltshire night.

O housewife safe in the comprehensive churning
  Of the Warminster launderette!
O husband down at the depot with car in car-park!
  The Halt is waiting yet.

And when all the horrible roads are finally done for,
  And there's no more petrol left in the world to burn,
Here to the Halt from Salisbury and from Bristol
  Steam trains will return.

Harvest Hymn

We spray the fields and scatter
   The poison on the ground
So that no wicked wild flowers
   Upon our farm be found.
We like whatever helps us
   To line our purse with pence;
The twenty-four-hour broiler-house
   And neat electric fence.

All concrete sheds around us
   And Jaguars in the yard,
The telly lounge and deep-freeze
   Are ours from working hard.

We fire the fields for harvest,
   The hedges swell the flame,
The oak trees and the cottages
   From which our fathers came.
We give no compensation,
   The earth is ours today,
And if we lose on arable,
   Then bungalows will pay.

   All concrete sheds . . . etc.

Inexpensive Progress

Encase your legs in nylons,
Bestride your hills with pylons
    O age without a soul;
Away with gentle willows
And all the elmy billows
    That through your valleys roll.

Let's say good-bye to hedges
And roads with grassy edges
    And winding country lanes;
Let all things travel faster
Where motor-car is master
    Till only Speed remains.

Destroy the ancient inn-signs
But strew the roads with tin signs
    'Keep Left,' 'M4,' 'Keep Out!'
Command, instruction, warning,
Repetitive adorning
    The rockeried roundabout;

For every raw obscenity
Must have its small 'amenity,'
    Its patch of shaven green,
And hoardings look a wonder
In banks of floribunda
    With floodlights in between.

Leave no old village standing
Which could provide a landing
    For aeroplanes to roar,
But spare such cheap defacements
As huts with shattered casements
    Unlived-in since the war.

Let no provincial High Street
Which might be your or my street
    Look as it used to do,
But let the chain stores place here
Their miles of black glass facia
    And traffic thunder through.

And if there is some scenery,
Some unpretentious greenery,
    Surviving anywhere,
It does not need protecting
For soon we'll be erecting
    A Power Station there.

When all our roads are lighted
By concrete monsters sited
    Like gallows overhead,
Bathed in the yellow vomit
Each monster belches from it,
    We'll know that we are dead.

The Village Inn

'The village inn, the dear old inn,
So ancient, clean and free from sin,
True centre of our rural life
Where Hodge sits down beside his wife
And talks of Marx and nuclear fission
With all a rustic's intuition.
Ah, more than church or school or hall,
The village inn's the heart of all.'
So spake the brewer's P.R.O.,
A man who really ought to know,
For he is paid for saying so.
And then he kindly gave to me
A lovely coloured booklet free.
'Twas full of prose that sang the praise
Of coaching inns in Georgian days,
Showing how public-houses are
More modern than the motor-car,
More English than the weald or wold
And almost equally as old,
And run for love and not for gold
Until I felt a filthy swine
For loathing beer and liking wine,
And rotten to the very core
And thinking village inns a bore,
And village bores more sure to roam
To village inns than stay at home.
And then I thought I *must* be wrong,
So up I rose and went along
To that old village alehouse where
In neon lights is written 'Bear'.

Ah, where's the inn that once I knew
    With brick and chalky wall
Up which the knobbly pear-tree grew
    For fear the place would fall?

Oh, that old pot-house isn't there,
    It wasn't worth our while;
You'll find we have rebuilt 'The Bear'
    In Early Georgian style.

But winter jasmine used to cling
    With golden stars a-shine
Where rain and wind would wash and swing
    The crudely painted sign.

And where's the roof of golden thatch?
    The chimney-stack of stone?
The crown-glass panes that used to match
    Each sunset with their own?

Oh now the walls are red and smart,
    The roof has emerald tiles.
The neon sign's a work of art
    And visible for miles.

The bar inside was papered green,
    The settles grained like oak,
The only light was paraffin,
    The woodfire used to smoke.

And photographs from far and wide
    Were hung around the room:
The hunt, the church, the football side,
    And Kitchener of Khartoum.

Our air-conditioned bars are lined
  With washable material,
The stools are steel, the taste refined,
  Hygienic and ethereal.

Hurrah, hurrah, for hearts of oak!
  Away with inhibitions!
For here's a place to sit and soak
  In sanit'ry conditions.

Slough

Come, friendly bombs, and fall on Slough
It isn't fit for humans now,
There isn't grass to graze a cow
  Swarm over, Death!

Come, bombs, and blow to smithereens
Those air-conditioned, bright canteens,
Tinned fruit, tinned meat, tinned milk, tinned beans
  Tinned minds, tinned breath.

Mess up the mess they call a town –
A house for ninety-seven down
And once a week a half-a-crown
  For twenty years,

And get that man with double chin
Who'll always cheat and always win,
Who washes his repulsive skin
   In women's tears,

And smash his desk of polished oak
And smash his hands so used to stroke
And stop his boring dirty joke
   And make him yell.

But spare the bald young clerks who add
The profits of the stinking cad;
It's not their fault that they are mad,
   They've tasted Hell.

It's not their fault they do not know
The birdsong from the radio,
It's not their fault they often go
   To Maidenhead

And talk of sports and makes of cars
In various bogus Tudor bars
And daren't look up and see the stars
   But belch instead.

In labour-saving homes, with care
Their wives frizz out peroxide hair
And dry it in synthetic air
   And paint their nails.

Come, friendly bombs, and fall on Slough
To get it ready for the plough.
The cabbages are coming now;
   The earth exhales.

Cornish Cliffs

Those moments, tasted once and never done,
Of long surf breaking in the mid-day sun.
A far-off blow-hole booming like a gun –

The seagulls plane and circle out of sight
Below this thirsty, thrift-encrusted height,
The veined sea-campion buds burst into white

And gorse turns tawny orange, seen beside
Pale drifts of primroses cascading wide
To where the slate falls sheer into the tide.

More than in gardened Surrey, nature spills
A wealth of heather, kidney-vetch and squills
Over these long-defended Cornish hills.

A gun-emplacement of the latest war
Looks older than the hill fort built before
Saxon or Norman headed for the shore.

And in the shadowless, unclouded glare
Deep blue above us fades to whiteness where
A misty sea-line meets the wash of air.

Nut-smell of gorse and honey-smell of ling
Waft out to sea the freshness of the spring
On sunny shallows, green and whispering.

The wideness which the lark-song gives the sky
Shrinks at the clang of sea-birds sailing by
Whose notes are tuned to days when seas are high.

From today's calm, the lane's enclosing green
Leads inland to a usual Cornish scene –
Slate cottages with sycamore between,

Small fields and tellymasts and wires and poles
With, as the everlasting ocean rolls,
Two chapels built for half a hundred souls.

Hunter Trials

It's awf'lly bad luck on Diana,
   Her ponies have swallowed their bits;
She fished down their throats with a spanner
   And frightened them all into fits.

So now she's attempting to borrow.
   Do lend her some bits, Mummy, *do*;
I'll lend her my own for to-morrow,
   But to-day *I*'ll be wanting them too.

Just look at Prunella on Guzzle,
   The wizardest pony on earth;
Why doesn't she slacken his muzzle
   And tighten the breech in his girth?

I say, Mummy, there's Mrs Geyser
    And doesn't she look pretty sick?
I bet it's because Mona Lisa
    Was hit on the hock with a brick.

Miss Blewitt says Monica threw it,
    But Monica says it was Joan,
And Joan's very thick with Miss Blewitt,
    So Monica's sulking alone.

And Margaret failed in her paces,
    Her withers got tied in a noose,
So her coronets caught in the traces
    And now all her fetlocks are loose.

Oh, it's me now. I'm terribly nervous.
    I wonder if Smudges will shy.
She's practically certain to swerve as
    Her Pelham is over one eye.

*   *   *

Oh wasn't it naughty of Smudges?
    Oh, Mummy, I'm sick with disgust.
She threw me in front of the Judges,
    And my silly old collarbone's bust.

A Subaltern's Love-song

Miss J. Hunter Dunn, Miss J. Hunter Dunn,
Furnish'd and burnish'd by Aldershot sun,
What strenuous singles we played after tea,
We in the tournament – you against me!

Love-thirty, love-forty, oh! weakness of joy,
The speed of a swallow, the grace of a boy,
With carefullest carelessness, gaily you won,
I am weak from your loveliness, Joan Hunter Dunn.

Miss Joan Hunter Dunn, Miss Joan Hunter Dunn,
How mad I am, sad I am, glad that you won.
The warm-handled racket is back in its press,
But my shock-headed victor, she loves me no less.

Her father's euonymus shines as we walk,
And swing past the summer-house, buried in talk,
And cool the verandah that welcomes us in
To the six-o'clock news and a lime-juice and gin.

The scent of the conifers, sound of the bath,
The view from my bedroom of moss-dappled path,
As I struggle with double-end evening tie,
For we dance at the Golf Club, my victor and I.

On the floor of her bedroom lie blazer and shorts
And the cream-coloured walls are be-trophied with
    sports,
And westering, questioning settles the sun
On your low-leaded window, Miss Joan Hunter Dunn.

The Hillman is waiting, the light's in the hall,
The pictures of Egypt are bright on the wall,
My sweet, I am standing beside the oak stair
And there on the landing's the light on your hair.

By roads 'not adopted', by woodlanded ways,
She drove to the club in the late summer haze,
Into nine-o'clock Camberley, heavy with bells
And mushroomy, pine-woody, evergreen smells.

Miss Joan Hunter Dunn, Miss Joan Hunter Dunn,
I can hear from the car-park the dance has begun.
Oh! full Surrey twilight! importunate band!
Oh! strongly adorable tennis-girl's hand!

Around us are Rovers and Austins afar,
Above us, the intimate roof of the car,
And here on my right is the girl of my choice,
With the tilt of her nose and the chime of her voice,

And the scent of her wrap, and the words never said,
And the ominous, ominous dancing ahead.
We sat in the car park till twenty to one
And now I'm engaged to Miss Joan Hunter Dunn.

How to Get On in Society

(originally set as a competition in 'Time and Tide')

Phone for the fish-knives, Norman
    As Cook is a little unnerved;
You kiddies have crumpled the serviettes
    And I must have things daintily served.

Are the requisites all in the toilet?
    The frills round the cutlets can wait
Till the girl has replenished the cruets
    And switched on the logs in the grate.

It's ever so close in the lounge, dear,
    But the vestibule's comfy for tea
And Howard is out riding on horseback
    So do come and take some with me.

Now here is a fork for your pastries
    And do use the couch for your feet;
I know what I wanted to ask you –
    Is trifle sufficient for sweet?

Milk and then just as it comes dear?
    I'm afraid the preserve's full of stones;
Beg pardon, I'm soiling the doileys
    With afternoon tea-cakes and scones.

Inland Waterway

(declaimed at the opening of the Upper Avon at Stratford in the presence of the Queen Mother and Robert Aickman, founder of the Inland Waterways Association, on 1 June 1974)

He who by peaceful inland water steers
Bestirs himself when a new lock appears.
Slow swing the gates: slow sinks the water down;
This lower Stratford seems another town.
The meadows which the youthful Shakespeare knew
Are left behind, and, sliding into view,
Come reaches of the Avon, mile on mile,
Church, farm and mill and lover-leaned-on stile,
Till where the tower of Tewkesbury soars to heaven
Our homely Avon joins the haughty Severn.
Sweet is the fluting of the blackbird's note,
Sweet is the ripple from the narrow boat.

Your Majesty, our friend of many years,
Confirms a triumph now the moment nears:
The lock you have re-opened will set free
The heart of England to the open sea.

Beaumaris
December 21, 1963

(It was a Christmas-tide custom at Beaumaris, Anglesey, for the Queen of the Hunt Ball to throw heated halfpence from a shovel to the crowd below.)

Low-shot light of a sharp December
  Shifting, lifted a morning haze:
Opening fans of smooth sea-water
  Touched in silence the tiny bays:
In bright Beaumaris the people waited –
  This was Laurelie's day of days.

At the northern end of the street a vista
  Of sunlit woodland; and south, a tower;
Across the water from Hansom's terrace,
  The glass'd reflection of Penmaenmawr:
High on her balcony Laurelie Williams
  Waved the shovel and shot the shower.

Down on us all fell heated ha'pence,
  Up to her all of us looked for more:
Laurelie Williams, Laurelie Williams –
  Lovelier now than ever before
With your straight black hair and your fresh complexion:
  Diamond-bright was the brooch you wore.

Life be kind to you, Laurelie Williams,
  With girlhood over and marriage begun:
Queuing for buses and rearing children,
  Washing the dishes and missing the fun,
May you still recall how you flung the coppers
  On bright Beaumaris in winter sun.

Death in Leamington

She died in the upstairs bedroom
    By the light of the ev'ning star
That shone through the plate glass window
    From over Leamington Spa.

Beside her the lonely crochet
    Lay patiently and unstirred,
But the fingers that would have work'd it
    Were dead as the spoken word.

And Nurse came in with the tea-things
    Breast high 'mid the stands and chairs –
But Nurse was alone with her own little soul,
    And the things were alone with theirs.

She bolted the big round window,
    She let the blinds unroll,
She set a match to the mantle,
    She covered the fire with coal.

And 'Tea!' she said in a tiny voice
    'Wake up! It's nearly *five.*'
Oh! Chintzy, chintzy cheeriness,
    Half dead and half alive!

Do you know that the stucco is peeling?
    Do you know that the heart will stop?
From those yellow Italianate arches
    Do you hear the plaster drop?

Nurse looked at the silent bedstead,
  At the gray, decaying face,
As the calm of a Leamington ev'ning
  Drifted into the place.

She moved the table of bottles
  Away from the bed to the wall;
And tiptoeing gently over the stairs
  Turned down the gas in the hall.

Elizabeth Jennings

About the poet

Elizabeth Jennings was born in Lincolnshire in 1926 but has lived most of her life in Oxford. She has gained renown as a critic and anthologist, and as a translator of the sonnets of the artist Michelangelo, some of which can be found in her *Collected Poems* (1967). For her own writing she has been awarded both the Somerset Maugham Award and the W.H. Smith Literary Award.

Jennings's earlier published poetry is very personal and deals in a starkly open way with the time she had spent in hospital following a mental breakdown (*Recoveries* (1964) and *The Mind has Mountains* (1966)). The themes of suffering and loneliness continue into later volumes of her work – *Lucidities* (1970), *Moments of Grace* (1979) – and she explores religious faith, art, nature and the environment in these and her collection *Times and Seasons* (1992). She appears regularly on radio and television, gives public readings of her work and continues to write for national periodicals.

Parts of Speech

I Verb

Listen, the acute verb
Is linking subject and object –
Hear the links fall in place
And the sturdy padlock clinking.

A verb is a power in all speech,
Rings through prose and verse.
It brings to birth. Can't you hear
The first cry of awareness?

'I go', 'I forget', 'I exist'
By language only and always.
Blood cannot beat in a void
And the potent, fiery tongue

Offers the gift of language,
Blesses our lips and throats.
'I love you' vows and connects
And moves in a climate of tensions.

II Adjective

I'm a close relative
    Of nouns, I reinforce
Their moods and meanings, I live
    By running on a course

They also move on. I
    Live by music too,
The run and scheme and cry
    That rises to the blue

Taut skies. I qualify
    And temper every noun,
Enrich it, help it fly.
    I'm never on my own.

Say 'Love' and you must add
    'Sweet love', 'dear love' and make
Your message deeper, lead
    To love for its rich sake.

III Noun

I preen myself, I am a peacock word,
    I am a call, am one
Who does not need a tether or a cord,
    I dally in the sun

And in the life of grammar take a part
    That is a main one. You
Can never do without me. I'm the heart
    And teller of what's true.

IV Adverb

I qualify, I add to, I insist
   That verbs are active, go
About their business aptly. I exist
   Mainly to let them show

How graceful and how many-natured are
   Their meanings and their tense
Purposes. I show them how to wear
   Any experience

With a fine gesture. Yet I also can
   Help them to hide and go
Into small cells where they tell what a man
   Can shape alone. I show

Verbs they are needy on their busy own.
   I hand right clothes out and
Help them to speak a need or use a phone
   And how to understand.

A Question of Form

The point is that a Monet does not move,
A Mozart clarinet sonata can't
Be seen or smelt. Art works by metaphor
And cool constriction. Cool means white-hot here.
By rule and lack of liberty art's meant

To work and at its best it does so. Last
Tuesday I was heckled by a boy
Who said that poetry never should be cast
In form, but come without control and fast.
I knew that all this had to do with joy

And pleasure. Why did I not think to say
Nature has limitations? Trees can't move
Away from roots. They only grow that way.
I said 'Form's not a jelly-mould to pour
A poem into. It can only say
Whatever is its message.' But I saw

That none of this convinced, yet Baudelaire
Juggled the senses. Language smelt and could
Taste, but still switched senses had to say
Their mood and tone in form. All art can play
But always is contained, leashed in. The good
Work of art makes laws it must obey.

The Enemies

Last night they came across the river and
Entered the city. Women were awake
With lights and food. They entertained the band,
Not asking what the men had come to take
Or what strange tongue they spoke
Or why they came so suddenly through the land.

Now in the morning all the town is filled
With stories of the swift and dark invasion;
The women say that not one stranger told
A reason for his coming. The intrusion
Was not for devastation:
Peace is apparent still on hearth and field.

Yet all the city is a haunted place.
Man meeting man speaks cautiously. Old friends
Close up the candid looks upon their face.
There is no warmth in hands accepting hands;
Each ponders, 'Better hide myself in case
Those strangers have set up their homes in minds
I used to walk in. Better draw the blinds
Even if the strangers haunt in my own house.'

Old Woman

So much she caused she cannot now account for
As she stands watching day return, the cool
Walls of the house moving towards the sun.
She puts some flowers in a vase and thinks
    'There is not much I can arrange
In here and now, but flowers are suppliant

As children never were. And love is now
A flicker of memory, my body is
My own entirely. When I lie at night
I gather nothing now into my arms,
    No child or man, and where I live
Is what remains when men and children go.'

Yet she owns more than residue of lives
That she has marked and altered. See how she
Warns time from too much touching her possessions
By keeping flowers fed, by polishing
    Her fine old silver. Gratefully
She sees her own glance printed on grandchildren.

Drawing the curtains back and opening windows
Every morning now, she feels her years
Grow less and less. Time puts no burden on
Her now she does not need to measure it.
    It is acceptance she arranges
And her own life she places in the vase.

Old Man

His age drawn out behind him to be watched:
It is his shadow you may say. That dark
He paints upon the wall is his past self,
A mark he only leaves when he is still
    And he is still now always,
At ease and watching all his life assemble.

And he intends nothing but watching. What
His life has made of him his shadow shows –
Fine graces gone but dignity remaining,
While all he shuffled after is composed
    Into a curve of dark, of silences:
An old man tranquil in his silences.

And we move round him, are his own world turning,
Spinning it seems to him, leaving no shadow
To blaze our trail. We are our actions only:
He is himself, abundant and assured,
    All action thrown away,
And time is slowing where his shadow stands.

My Grandmother

She kept an antique shop – or it kept her.
Among Apostle spoons and Bristol glass,
The faded silks, the heavy furniture,
She watched her own reflection in the brass
Salvers and silver bowls, as if to prove
Polish was all, there was no need of love.

And I remember how I once refused
To go out with her, since I was afraid.
It was perhaps a wish not to be used
Like antique objects. Though she never said
That she was hurt, I still could feel the guilt
Of that refusal, guessing how she felt.

Later, too frail to keep a shop, she put
All her best things in one long narrow room.
The place smelt old, of things too long kept shut,
The smell of absences where shadows come
That can't be polished. There was nothing then
To give her own reflection back again.

And when she died I felt no grief at all,
Only the guilt of what I once refused.
I walked into her room among the tall
Sideboards and cupboards – things she never used
But needed: and no finger-marks were there,
Only the new dust falling through the air.

For My Mother

I My Mother Dying Aged 87

You died as quietly as your spirit moved
All through my life. It was a shock to hear
Your shallow breathing and more hard to see
Your eyes closed fast. You did not wake for me
But even so I do not shed a tear.
Your spirit has flown free

Of that small shell of flesh. Grandchildren stood
Quietly by and it was they who gave
Most strength to us. They also loved you for
Your gentleness. You never made them fear
Anything. The memories you leave
Are happy times. You were

The one who gave me stamps and envelopes
And posted all my early poems. You had
Such faith in me. You could be firm and would
Curb tantrums, and would change an angry mood
With careful threats. I cannot feel too sad
Today for you were good

And that is what the kindly letters say.
Some are clumsy, some embarrass with
Lush piety but all will guide your ship
Upon a calm, bright ocean and we keep
Our eyes on it. It is too strong for death
And so we do not weep.

Song at the Beginning of Autumn

Now watch this autumn that arrives
In smells. All looks like summer still;
Colours are quite unchanged, the air
On green and white serenely thrives.
Heavy the trees with growth and full
The fields. Flowers flourish everywhere.

Proust who collected time within
A child's cake would understand
The ambiguity of this –
Summer still raging while a thin
Column of smoke stirs from the land
Proving that autumn gropes for us.

But every season is a kind
Of rich nostalgia. We give names –
Autumn and summer, winter, spring –
As though to unfasten from the mind
Our moods and give them outward forms.
We want the certain, solid thing.

But I am carried back against
My will into a childhood where
Autumn is bonfires, marbles, smoke;
I lean against my window fenced
From evocations in the air.
When I said autumn, autumn broke.

The Smell of Chrysanthemums

The chestnut leaves are toasted. Conkers spill
Upon the pavements. Gold is vying with
Yellow, ochre, brown. There is a feel
Of dyings and departures. Smoky breath
 Rises and I know how Winter comes
 When I can smell the rich chrysanthemums.

It is so poignant and it makes me mourn
For what? The going year? The sun's eclipse?
All these and more. I see the dead leaves burn
And everywhere the Summer lies in heaps.
 I close my eyes and feel how Winter comes
 With acrid incense of chrysanthemums.

I shall not go to school again and yet
There's an old sadness that disturbs me most.
The nights come early; every bold sunset
Tells me that Autumn soon will be a ghost,
 But I know best how Winter always comes
 In the wide scent of strong chrysanthemums.

Lazarus

It was the amazing white, it was the way he simply
Refused to answer our questions, it was the cold pale
  glance
Of death upon him, the smell of death that truly
Declared his rising to us. It was no chance
Happening, as a man may fill a silence
Between two heart-beats, seem to be dead and then
Astonish us with the closeness of his presence;
This man was dead, I say it again and again.
All of our sweating bodies moved towards him
And our minds moved too, hungry for finished faith.
He would not enter our world at once with words
That we might be tempted to twist or argue with:
Cold like a white root pressed in the bowels of earth
He looked, but also vulnerable – like birth.

Love Poem

There is a shyness that we have
Only with those whom we most love.
Something it has to do also
With how we cannot bring to mind
A face whose every line we know.
O love is kind, O love is kind.

That there should still remain the first
Sweetness, also the later thirst –
This is why pain must play some part
In all true feelings that we find
And every shaking of the heart.
O love is kind, O love is kind.

And it is right that we should want
Discretion, secrecy, no hint
Of what we share. Love which cries out,
And wants the world to understand,
Is love that holds itself in doubt.
For love is quiet, and love is kind.

An Age of Doubt

They stay there on an impulse
A seed, a star, an explosion
And all creation followed on this, and design
Was really haphazard. I never shall believe it.
I stare tonight at a late-March sky and see stars
Distributed in patterns we have found
And named and taken over.
Atheists say with certainty all this started
By chance, that there's no maker.

Once, after a childhood full of trust
And hope and faith, I suddenly felt unsure,
Thought of the Holy Ghost as a huge bird
Which I knew did not exist.
After that, doubt followed doubt, nothing was certain,
I wanted my faith and trust back, longed for the sure
Days of childhood. They would not return.
For months, no, years, I lived in doubt. I read
Books of philosophy, they gave further doubts,
Ones I had never heard of.
This was the doubt of life, my late adolescence,
I thought that growing up meant loss of innocence,
Hated my altering body.
My mind, so wide once with imagined kingdoms,
Shrivelled and shrank to doubt of my own existence,
Let alone of God's or of another's.
My dear, delightful days of saying Mass,
Of moving in dreams of angels all about me
Disappeared and I was alone, one doubt
And not even sure of that.

Gradually, O so slowly and discreetly
Faith crept back, stars reappeared in patterns.
And what brought this about?
I was reading poems, falling in love with verse,
With Keats and his nightingale and Grecian urn,
With Coleridge and his Ancient Mariner,
Wordsworth near Tintern Abbey.
And soon I started to write my small attempts
At the art of verse. I entered a huge family,
A place where poetry sang and was applauded,
Where love was how a stanza whispered its way
Above a starlit forest,
And my rhythms tried to copy the tides' huge impulse,
Dover Beach, most of all.
And, unlike Matthew Arnold's, my waves came in
With ships of certainty putting their anchors down
And settling in the jetties of *my* country,
And I gazed at the full and half and quarter-moon
And the stars all seemed to surrender to obvious music
Conjured by poets making a potent song.
So I began to feel a little, O such a little
But so authentic a power, it altered my poems
Whose rhythms sometimes moved to the tide of creation
And felt the touch of a God.

Wendy Cope

About the poet

Wendy Cope was born in Erith, Kent (now part of Greater London) in 1945. She attended boarding school and then St Hilda's College, Oxford, where she read History. From Oxford she moved to London where she taught in a primary school for fifteen years, before becoming a full-time writer.

Although she admits to not having been fond of poetry at primary school: 'The poems we did at junior school were mostly about nature and fairies. "Who has seen the wind?" nearly put me off Christina Rossetti for life', things changed later: 'poetry improved when we began working on the . . . English Literature syllabus. I was surprised to find out how much I liked certain poems by Yeats, Hardy and James Elroy Flecker. In the sixth form . . . I was bowled over by Keats.'

Rediscovering poetry in her twenties, Wendy Cope has gone on to write parodies, pastiches and personal, autobiographical poems, and won the Cholmondeley Award for Poetry in 1987. She has been described as 'wise, funny, artful, subversive' and is one of Britain's best-known contemporary poets, writing regularly for newspapers and magazines and speaking in schools and colleges throughout Britain. Her collections include **Making Cocoa for Kingsley Amis** (1986) and **Serious Concerns** (1992), and she has also written a long narrative poem, **The River Girl** (1991).

Tich Miller

Tich Miller wore glasses
with elastoplast-pink frames
and had one foot three sizes larger then the other.

When they picked teams for outdoor games
she and I were always the last two
left standing by the wire-mesh fence.

We avoided one another's eyes,
stooping, perhaps, to re-tie a shoelace,
or affecting interest in the flight

of some fortunate bird, and pretended
not to hear the urgent conference:
'Have Tubby!' 'No, no, have Tich!'

Usually they chose me, the lesser dud,
and she lolloped, unselected,
to the back of the other team.

At eleven we went to different schools.
In time I learned to get my own back,
sneering at hockey-players who couldn't spell.

Tich died when she was twelve.

Lizzy

The night that Lizzy swallowed all her aspirins
She hadn't spent the evening on her own, nor
Trying vainly to impress the man she loved,
But with the one she didn't want, the kindly
Pink-faced youth who would have married her.

I understood her then – the way a senseless
Chain of unrequited love makes matters worse,
And knowing how we feel about
The ones we disappoint, their company
As welcome as an insect in the eye.

Lizzy survived the aspirins, two gas-filled rooms
And other graceful blonds she couldn't win.
At last she married someone not unlike
The pink-faced youth – she says she's happy
And I don't ask questions. We can't talk much any more.

For My Sister, Emigrating

You've left with me
the things you couldn't take
or bear to give away –
books, records and a biscuit-tin
that Nanna gave you.

It's old and dirty
and the lid won't fit.
Standing in a corner of my room,
quite useless, it's as touching
as a once loved toy.

Yes, sentimental now –
but if you'd stayed,
we would have quarrelled
just the same as ever,
found excuses not to phone.

We never learn. We've grown up
struggling, frightened
that the family would drown us,
only giving in to love
when someone's dead or gone.

Names

She was Eliza for a few weeks
When she was a baby –
Eliza Lily. Soon it changed to Lil.

Later she was Miss Steward in the baker's shop
And then 'my love', 'my darling', Mother.

Widowed at thirty, she went back to work
As Mrs Hand. Her daughter grew up,
Married and gave birth.

Now she was Nanna. 'Everybody
Calls me Nanna,' she would say to visitors.
And so they did – friends, tradesmen, the doctor.

In the geriatric ward
They used the patients' Christian names.
'Lil,' we said, 'or Nanna,'
But it wasn't in her file
And for those last bewildered weeks
She was Eliza once again.

Engineers' Corner

Why isn't there an Engineers' Corner in Westminster Abbey?
In Britain we've always made more fuss of a ballad than a blueprint
. . . How many schoolchildren dream of becoming great engineers?
Advertisement placed in The Times *by the Engineering Council*

We make more fuss of ballads than of blueprints –
That's why so many poets end up rich,
While engineers scrape by in cheerless garrets.
Who needs a bridge or dam? Who needs a ditch?

Whereas the person who can write a sonnet
Has got it made. It's always been the way,
For everybody knows that we need poems
And everybody reads them every day.

Yes, life is hard if you choose engineering –
You're sure to need another job as well;
You'll have to plan your projects in the evenings
Instead of going out. It must be hell.

While well-heeled poets ride around in Daimlers,
You'll burn the midnight oil to earn a crust,
With no hope of a statue in the Abbey,
With no hope, even, of a modest bust.

No wonder small boys dream of writing couplets
And spurn the bike, the lorry and the train.
There's far too much encouragement for poets –
That's why this country's going down the drain.

Does She Like Word-Games?

She likes sonnets but she doesn't like poems.
She doesn't like sestinas or whisky.
No, she doesn't like limericks either, or water, or
    television or cats.

She likes sweets but she doesn't like eating.
She likes apples too.

She likes Schumann but she doesn't like Stravinsky.
She's fond of jazz and piccolos.
She dislikes songs.

She has a warm regard for Russian dancers,
Spanish jugglers, little people,
Especially if they're green.

She likes especially as well. And as well
For that matter. And for that matter.
She can't stand Shakespeare.

Among her favourites are spelling bees,
Football, the Book of Common Prayer.
And there are great loves –
James Russell Lowell, the Mississippi.

She likes sonnets but she doesn't like the sky.

She doesn't like repetition.
She doesn't like repetition.

She doesn't like endings.

A Christmas Carol

We three ships of Bethlehem are,
Ox and ass sing 'Gloria',
Church bells kneeling, shepherds peeling,
Lullay thou little star.

Chorus:

Oh, silent David, darkest light,
Choirs of holly in the night,
New-born story, merry glory,
May thy puddings all be bright.

Hark! the shining gentlemen sing,
Lo! the infant seraphim ring,
Hither ages, through the pages,
Manger on the wing.

Come thou pine logs from on high,
Praise the happy Christmas pie,
Yonder present, bearing peasant,
Wassailing in the sky.

Mild the stable, bitter the sound,
Incense cradled on the ground,
Winds a-glowing, tidings blowing
Holiness all around.

19th Christmas Poem

for Nicholas Shakespeare and John Coldstream

Christmas is coming.
The phone rings and I curse.
Literary editor.
Seasonal verse.

Big deal. Big chance
To sell them a rhyme.
They never publish poetry
Except at Christmas-time.

Christmas is coming,
Last week in September.
Can you let us have it
By the second of November?

Light and clean and printable –
You know the kind of thing.
If you want a Christmas bonus,
Now's the time to sing.

Christmas is coming.
Books of the year.
I re-read *Persuasion*,
War and Peace, King Lear.

We don't count that stuff.
It isn't what we mean.
We thought you were part
Of the literary scene.

Christmas is coming.
Better play the game.
Mother reads the *Telegraph*.
She likes to see my name.

Last year it made her
Happy as a bird
To find her elder daughter
Under Douglas Hurd.

Christmas is coming.
Here's my Christmas song –
Light and clean and printable
And forty lines long.

Dear Dial-a-poet,
Hope it will do.
Please to pay without delay
And God bless you.

Manifesto

I'll work, for there's new purpose in my art –
I'll muster all my talent, all my wit
And write the poems that will win your heart.

Pierced by a rusty allegoric dart,
What can I do but make the best of it?
I'll work, for there's new purpose in my art.

You're always on my mind when we're apart –
I can't afford to daydream, so I'll sit
And write the poems that will win your heart.

I am no beauty but I'm pretty smart
And I intend to be your favourite –
I'll work, for there's new purpose in my art.

And if some bloodless literary fart
Says that it's all too personal, I'll spit
And write the poems that will win your heart.

I feel terrific now I've made a start –
I'll have another book before I quit.
I'll work, for there's new purpose in my art,
And write the poems that will win your heart.

A Nursery Rhyme

as it might have been written by William Wordsworth

The skylark and the jay sang loud and long,
The sun was calm and bright, the air was sweet,
When all at once I heard above the throng
Of jocund birds a single plaintive bleat.

And, turning, saw, as one sees in a dream,
It was a Sheep had broke the moorland peace
With his sad cry, a creature who did seem
The blackest thing that ever wore a fleece.

I walked towards him on the stony track
And, pausing for a while between two crags,
I asked him, 'Have you wool upon your back?'
Thus he bespake, 'Enough to fill three bags.'

Most courteously, in measured tones, he told
Who would receive each bag and where they dwelt;
And oft, now years have passed and I am old,
I recollect with joy that inky pelt.

The Cricketing Versions

for Simon Rae

'There isn't much cricket in the Cromwell play'
(overheard at a dinner-party)

There isn't much cricket in *Hamlet* either,
There isn't much cricket in *Lear*.
I don't think there's any in *Paradise Lost** –
I haven't a copy right here.

But I like to imagine the cricketing versions –
Laertes goes out to bat
And instead of claiming a palpable hit,
The prince gives a cry of 'Howzat!'

While elsewhere the nastier daughters of Lear
(Both women cricketers) scheme
To keep their talented younger sister
Out of the England team,

And up in the happy realms of light
When Satan is out (great catch)
His team and the winners sit down together
For sandwiches after the match.

*Apparently there is. 'Chaos umpire sits,/And by decision
more embroils the fray.' *Paradise Lost*, Book II, lines 907–8.

Although there are some English writers
Who feature the red leather ball,
You could make a long list of the plays and the books
In which there's no cricket at all.

To be perfectly honest, I like them that way –
The absence of cricket is fine.
But if you prefer work that includes it, please note
That now there's some cricket in mine.

Strugnell's Haiku

(i)

The cherry blossom
In my neighbour's garden – Oh!
It looks really nice.

(ii)

The leaves have fallen
And the snow has fallen and
Soon my hair also . . . . .

(iii)

November evening:
The moon is up, rooks settle,
The pubs are open.

Strugnell's Sonnets

(iv)

Not only marble, but the plastic toys
From cornflake packets will outlive this rhyme:
I can't immortalize you, love – our joys
Will lie unnoticed in the vault of time.
When Mrs Thatcher has been cast in bronze
And her administration is a page
In some O-level text-book, when the dons
Have analysed the story of our age,
When travel firms sell tours of outer space
And aeroplanes take off without a sound
And Tulse Hill has become a trendy place
And Upper Norwood's on the underground
Your beauty and my name will be forgotten –
My love is true, but all my verse is rotten.

(vi)

Let me not to the marriage of true swine
Admit impediments. With his big car
He's won your heart, and you have punctured mine.
I have no spare; henceforth I'll bear the scar.
Since women are not worth the booze you buy them
I dedicate myself to Higher Things.
If men deride and sneer, I shall defy them
And soar above Tulse Hill on poet's wings –
A brother to the thrush in Brockwell Park,
Whose song, though sometimes drowned by rock guitars,
Outlives their din. One day I'll make my mark,
Although I'm not from Ulster or from Mars,
And when I'm published in some classy mag
You'll rue the day you scarpered in his Jag.

Gillian Clarke

About the poet

Born in Cardiff in 1937, Gillian Clarke still lives and works in her native Wales. She was for some time editor of the *Anglo-Welsh Review* and now works as a freelance writer. She also lectures to adults and teaches creative writing to children in primary schools and to secondary school students. One of her projects was a sequence of poems, *The King of Britain's Daughter*, commissioned for the 1993 Hay-on-Wye Literary Festival.

Much of Clarke's poetry takes its inspiration from the themes of legend, while her imagery evokes the landscape and wildlife of rural Wales and middle Britain. The use of imagery is an important feature of her writing and she teaches children that: 'You can do anything with images. A poet can make anything, do anything, make us see, hear, feel, smell, taste, imagine anything that he or she wants.'

Other volumes available by Gillian Clarke are *Selected Poems* (1985) and *Letting in the Rumour* (1989).

Stealing Peas

Tamp of a clean ball on stretched gut.
Warm evening voices over clipped privet.
Cut grass. Saltfish from the mudflats,
and the tide far out.

He wore a blue shirt with an Aertex logo,
filthy with syrups of laurel and rhododendron,
the grime of a town park.
We crawled in the pea-rows
in a stolen green light,
pea-curls catching the tendrils of my hair,
peas tight in their pods as sucklers.
We slit the skins with bitten nails,
and slid the peas down the chutes of our tongues.
The little ones were sweet,
the big ones dusty and bitter.

'Who d'you like best?'
Beyond the freckled light of the allotment,
the strawberry beds, the pigeon cotes,
a lawn-mower murmured, and the parky shouted
at a child we could not see.

'You're prettier. She's funnier.'
I wished I hadn't asked.

The Vet

'Would the child like to leave?
It won't be pleasant.'

But I'm stuck with it,
brazening out the cowshed
and the chance of horror,
not knowing how to leave
once I'd said I'd stay.

Gloved to the elbow in blood
and her mysterious collar of muscle,
he wrenched from the deep cathedral of her belly
where her heart hung and the calf swam in its pool,
a long bellowing howl
and a rope of water.

I got off lightly that time,
no knife, no severing,
no inter-uterine butchery
to cut them free.

He let go the rope of water
and the calf swam home like a salmon
furled in a waterfall,
gleaming, silver, sweet under the tongue
of his brimming mother.

Anorexic

My father's sister,
the one who died
before there was a word for it,
was fussy with her food.
'Eat up,' they'd say to me,
ladling a bowl with warning.

What I remember's
how she'd send me to the dairy,
taught me to take cream,
the standing gold.
Where the jug dipped
I saw its blue-milk skin
before the surface healed.

Breath held, tongue between teeth,
I carried in the cream,
brimmed, level,
parallel, I knew,
with that other, hidden horizon
of the earth's deep
ungleaming water-table.

And she, more often than not half-dressed,
stockings, a slip, a Chinese kimono,
would warm the cream, pour it
with crumbled melting cheese
over a delicate white cauliflower,
or field mushrooms
steaming in porcelain,

then watch us eat, relishing,
smoking her umpteenth cigarette,
glamorous, perfumed, starved,
and going to die.

Musician

His carpet splattered like a Jackson Pollock
with clothes, books, instruments, the *NME*,
he strummed all day, read Beethoven sonatas.
He could hear it, he said, 'like words.'

That bitterest winter, he took up the piano, obsessed,
playing Bartok in the early hours. Snow fell,
veil after veil till we lost the car in the drive.
I slept under two duvets and my grandmother's fur,
and woke, suffocating, in the luminous nights
to hear the Hungarian Dances across moonlit snow.
The street cut off, immaculate, the house
glacial, suburbs hushed in wafery whiteness.
At dawn, hearing Debussy, I'd find him,
hands in fingerless gloves against the cold,
overcoat on. He hadn't gone to bed.

Snows banked the doors, rose to the sills,
silted the attic, drew veils across the windows.
Scent, sound, colour, detritus lay buried.
I dreamed the house vaulted and pillared with snow,
a drowned cathedral, waiting for the thaw,
and woke to hear the piano's muffled bells,
a first pianissimo slip of snow from the roof.

Swimming with Seals

Two horizons:
a far blue line where a ship
diminishes and the evening sun
lets slip;
and submarine
where we glimpse stars and shoals
and shadowy water-gardens
of what's beyond us.

When the seal rises
she rests her chin on the sea
as we do, and tames us with her gaze.
On shore the elderly
bask beside their cars
at the edge of what they've lost,
and shade their eyes
and lift binoculars.

She's gone,
apt to the sea's grace
to watch us underwater from her place,
you with your mask and fins,
strolling the shallow gardens of the sea,
me, finding depth
with a child's flounder of limbs,
hauling downwards on our chains of breath.

For a moment the old
looking out to sea,
all earth's weight beneath their folding chairs,
see only flawless blue to the horizon,
while we in seconds of caught air,
swim down against buoyancy,
rolling in amnion
like her September calf.

No Hands

War-planes have been at it all day long
shaking the world, strung air
humming like pianos when children bang the keys

over and over; willow warbler song
and jet planes; lads high on speed up there
in a mindless thrum; down here a brake of trees

churns to a rolling wave and there's no let
in the after-quiver along air-waves struck
by silly boys who think they strum guitars,

who skim the fields like surfboards over crests
of hedges, where a tractor swims in a green wake
of grass dust tossed to dry under sun and stars:

boy scaring boy off the face of his own land,
all do and dare, and look at me, no hands.

Lament

For the green turtle with her pulsing burden,
in search of the breeding ground.
For her eggs laid in their nest of sickness.

For the cormorant in his funeral silk,
the veil of iridescence on the sand,
the shadow on the sea.

For the ocean's lap with its mortal stain.
For Ahmed at the closed border.
For the soldier in his uniform of fire.

For the gunsmith and the armourer,
the boy fusilier who joined for the company,
the farmer's sons, in it for the music.

For the hook-beaked turtles,
the dugong and the dolphin,
the whale struck dumb by the missile's thunder.

For the tern, the gull and the restless wader,
the long migrations and the slow dying,
the veiled sun and the stink of anger.

For the burnt earth and the sun put out,
the scalded ocean and the blazing well.
For vengeance, and the ashes of language.

Neighbours

That spring was late. We watched the sky
and studied charts for shouldering isobars.
Birds were late to pair. Crows drank from the lamb's eye.

Over Finland small birds fell: song-thrushes
steering north, smudged signatures on light,
migrating warblers, nightingales.

Wing-beats failed over fjords, each lung a sip of gall.
Children were warned of their dangerous beauty.
Milk was spilt in Poland. Each quarrel

the blowback from some old story,
a mouthful of bitter air from the Ukraine
brought by the wind out of its box of sorrows.

This spring a lamb sips caesium on a Welsh hill.
A child, lifting her face to drink the rain,
takes into her blood the poisoned arrow.

Now we are all neighbourly, each little town
in Europe twinned to Chernobyl, each heart
with the burnt fireman, the child on the Moscow train.

In the democracy of the virus and the toxin
we wait. We watch for bird migrations,
one bird returning with green in its voice,

glasnost,
golau glas,
a first break of blue.

My Box

My box is made of golden oak,
my lover's gift to me.
He fitted hinges and a lock
of brass and a bright key.
He made it out of winter nights,
sanded and oiled and planed,
engraved inside the heavy lid
in brass, a golden tree.

In my box are twelve black books
where I have written down
how we have sanded, oiled and planed,
planted a garden, built a wall,
seen jays and goldcrests, rare red kites,
found the wild heartsease, drilled a well,
harvested apples and words and days
and planted a golden tree.

On an open shelf I keep my box.
Its key is in the lock.
I leave it there for you to read,
or them, when we are dead,
how everything is slowly made,
how slowly things made me,
a tree, a lover, words, a box,
books and a golden tree.

Red Poppy

from a painting by Georgia O'Keefe

'The meaning of a word
is not as exact
as the meaning of a colour'

So she walks out of the rectangles
of hard, crowded America
and floods the skies over southern plains

with carmine, scarlet,
with the swirl of poppy-silk.
There is music in it, and drumbeat.

You can put out the sun with poppy,
lie in long grass with beetle and ladybird
and shade your eyes with its awnings,

its heart of charcoal.
Wine glasses held to candles
or your veined lids against the sun.

The waters open for a million years,
petal after petal in the thundering river,
stamens of flying spray at its whirlpool heart.

Red mountain where the light slides
through the beating red of every Texan dusk,
and dark earth opens in a sooty yawn.

She paints out language, land, sky,
so we can only look and drown in deeps
of poppy under a thundering sun.

Lurcher

for Dylan

Dog of Rhygyfarch and Kells
hugely pacing the room and corridor,
turns on his heels
at invisible doors,

folds himself on the Indian rug
to a gilded initial. Oiled parts
rehearse in sleep,
loosing long golden farts

in great uncoilings that amaze and wake him,
his eyes' ringed planets towing moons of ice
out of the winter of a dream
at the far edge of space.

Brain too simple for his intricate body,
the spaniel shows him how to open doors.
He waits to go, patient, hind legs up and ready,
his beautiful head still down on lion forepaws.

Unleashed he flies,
illusion, hologram, he and his ghost
writing on air, on sand, two thousand years
of milgi in the gold rings of his eyes.

Peregrine Falcon

New blood in the killing-ground,
her scullery,
her boneyard.

I touch the raw wire
of vertigo
feet from the edge.

Her house is air. She comes downstairs
on a turn of wind.
This is her table.

She is arrow.
At two miles a minute
the pigeon bursts like a city.

While we turned our backs
she wasted nothing
but a rose-ringed foot

still warm.

◼ Glossary: reading the poems

15 *for Caribbean Independence*   'but also celebrates Africa's talking drums and their news-carrying function' (James Berry, page 15 of notes to **When I Dance**).

16 *a-galang*   going along.

  somody   somebody.

19 *the Creature*   Frankenstein's creation in Mary Shelley's novel.

20 *tawse*   strap used to mete out corporal punishment in schools.

21 *utility smocks*   type of clothing subsidised by the government in wartime to keep things affordable.

  helio sewing   embroidery.

22 *housing scheme*   council housing estate.

24 *peever*   hopscotch.

29 *Cenotaph*   monument to soldiers who are buried away from their own homes, in this case the one in Whitehall, London.

  forage cap   cap worn by soldiers when not on duty.

31 *something borrowed*   from an old rhyme that says brides should wear something old, new, borrowed and blue on their wedding day for good luck.

  Sugar Plums   boiled sweets; or possibly a reminder of the dance of the Sugar Plum fairy from the Nutcracker ballet.

32 *SWALK*   acronym for 'sealed with a loving kiss'.

  Amore   love (Italian).

33 *Guardian Personal Column*   on St Valentine's Day (14 February) each year the *Guardian* is one of several newspapers which carries an extended personal column just for lovers' greetings.

  Janet Reger   manufacturer of silk lingerie.

34 *Dreich*   boring, dreary (Scots).

   gloryhole   odds and ends box or room.

   to give . . . houseroom   find a place for.

38 *Lady Day*   25 March, Christian feast of the annunciation of the Blessed Virgin Mary.

39 *worsted*   fine woollen fabric.

   breast-pleat   front part of a shirt or smock.

42 *Tamar*   river which flows through Devon and Cornwall.

43 *Cotehele*   near Calstock, Cornwall, now a National Trust property.

   bonny   now means healthy-looking, but once meant strong.

   pass and ride   footpaths and bridleways.

44 *Sound*   Plymouth Sound.

45 *Henry Tudor*   eventually Henry VII.

46 *Bodrugan's Leap*   headland between Mevagissey and the Dodman, Cornwall.

47 *bruin*   name for a bear (used in the stories of Reynard the Fox).

49 *Dispensary*   place where medicines are dispensed; outpatients department; in the days prior to hospital treatment provided by the welfare state in Britain, those who could not afford treatment there visited the dispensary instead.

50 *year of the Revolution*   1917 – Russian Revolution.

   National School   the National Society was set up as a charity in 1811 with the aim of providing elementary schooling in England.

   Shell-shopped   Sid has mistaken the phrase 'shell-shocked'; many men returned from World War I with shell-shock, their minds seriously disturbed by the experience of war.

51 *the Somme*   river in northern France and region where, in World War I, the British and French fought the Germans in a series of battles from July to November 1916. Over one million soldiers died.

Lord George   Uncle probably means David Lloyd George (1863–1945), a British statesman who was described by Hitler as 'the man who won the [first] war'.

Kaiser Bill   Kaiser Wilhelm was a German emperor and remained as the country's figurehead throughout World War I, although he was forced to abdicate on 9 November 1918.

52 *chronic ward*   ward for patients with incurable illnesses.

53 *apoplexy*   an old-fashioned term, which usually refers to a brain haemorrhage or thrombosis.

54 *fractious charger*   angry war-horse.

55 *scat*   sudden shower.

56 *sodium*   older street lamps used a sodium vapour to give a yellow light.

60 *kyatta-pilla*   caterpillar (spelling indicates how the preacher pronounces it).

fufu   a kind of dough made from pounded plantains.

61 *Swahili/Yoruba*   Swahili – a Bantu language with some Arabic, spoken in Kenya, Tanzania and East Africa; Yoruba – a language of coastal West Africa.

nation language   Caribbean Creole, a dialect of English.

64 *slake*   drink down.

purgative   cleanser.

cochineal   a red dye, made from the crushed bodies of insects, and still used as a food colouring.

gauldings   type of bird, sometimes called egrets (Jamaican).

73 *Halt*   small, unattended railway station.

74 *broiler-house*   shed used for rearing chickens quickly.

75 *nylons*   stockings made from nylon, a synthetic fabric.

floribunda   group of plants, especially used when referring to a modern type of rose.

77 *Marx* Karl Marx (1818–83). A German political and social theorist famous for being the inspiration for modern Communism.

weald wooded countryside, from the Old English word *weald*.

wold open or upland country, from Old English *wald*, originally meaning forest.

78 *crown-glass* glass in windows which is made in circles, and looks like the bottom of a bottle.

Kitchener of Khartoum famous British military figure (1850–1916) who served in Africa and India and was appointed Secretary for War in 1914. He led the recruitment campaign for World War I and was figured prominently on posters declaring 'Your Country Needs You'.

79 *down* as a deposit.

80 *peroxide* hydrogen peroxide, a hair bleach that removes the natural colour.

81 *blow-hole* natural hole in the roof of a submerged cave. Air and water are forced up to the surface in a jet or spray as the tide comes in.

82 *bits* part of a bridle which the horse holds in its mouth.

83 *sick* (slang) disgusted.

very thick friendly.

traces straps used for leading the horse.

shy jump sideways through fear.

Pelham part of the bridle.

84 *Subaltern* officer below the rank of captain; a subordinate officer.

euonymus bush, sometimes known as the spindle tree.

double-end evening tie type of bow tie.

leaded window window where the lights, or small glass panes, are separated by strips of lead.

85 *'not adopted'* private road, common in rural areas; a road whose maintenance is paid for by the residents rather than by the local highways department.

86 'How to Get On in Society' was originally written for a competition and was then printed in a book by Nancy Mitford and others, **Noblesse Oblige**, in 1956. It was part of a debate on the differences between upper-class, or U English, and Non-U, and whether people were correct to choose certain words over others according to fashion. A good potted explanation can be found in David Crystal's **Encyclopaedia of Language**, pages 38–9, where a list of the two vocabulary styles is given.

cruets   jars holding salt, pepper, sauces and other condiments.

close   stuffy, stifling.

doileys   lace mats, or lacy paper mats sometimes put on to dishes.

88 *Beaumaris, Penmaenmawr*   towns on the north Wales coast.

Hansom's terrace   nineteenth-century houses designed by Joseph Hansom.

89 *mantle*   shade or hood on a gas lamp.

chintzy   literally covered with cheap, cheerful cotton cloth, but here used metaphorically.

90 *Turned down the gas*   dimmed the gas lamps.

95 *Monet*   Claude Monet, French Impressionist painter (1840–1926).

Mozart   Austrian composer (1756–91).

Baudelaire   Charles Baudelaire, French symbolist poet (1821–67).

99 *Apostle spoons*   silver spoons, often given to children at Christian baptism. The handles have figures of the apostles, the disciples of Christ, upon them.

101 *Proust . . . child's cake*   Marcel Proust, French novelist (1871–1922). His novel **Remembrance of Things Past** describes an incident in which he dips a small cake (a madeleine) into a cup of tea before he eats it. As he does so, memories of his childhood come flooding back to him, because he had done the same thing many times as a boy. Jennings, like Proust, is describing the way in which memories can be vividly brought back to us by the power of smells and tastes, however small and distant.

03 *Lazarus*   a man who was brought back to life after four days in his tomb by Christ. The story is told in the New Testament, John 11:1–44.

05 *Mass*   the celebration of the Lord's Supper in the Roman Catholic Church.

06 *Keats . . . nightingale and Grecian urn*   'Ode to a Nightingale' and 'Ode on a Grecian Urn', poems by John Keats (1795–1821).

Coleridge . . . Ancient Mariner   'The Rime of the Ancient Mariner', a poem by Samuel Taylor Coleridge (1772–1834).

Wordsworth near Tintern Abbey   'Tintern Abbey', a poem by William Wordsworth (1770–1850).

Dover Beach . . . Matthew Arnold   'Dover Beach', a poem by Matthew Arnold (1822–88).

12 *Engineers' Corner*   in Westminster Abbey there is a Poets' Corner where many literary figures are buried or have memorials erected to them.

well-heeled   wealthy.

13 *sestinas*   poem with six stanzas, each with six lines, and a final stanza of three lines.

Schumann . . . Stravinsky   Composers: Robert Schumann, German (1810–56); Igor Stravinsky, Russian-born (1882–1971).

James Russell Lowell   American poet and diplomat (1819–91).

16 *Douglas Hurd*   British politician (born in 1930).

17 *allegoric dart*   an arrow which represents the pain of love; in paintings and poetry of earlier centuries, Cupid, the mythological god of love, was supposed to wound people with his arrow. Once wounded, a person was bound to fall in love.

19 *Paradise Lost*   an epic poem about God's decision to throw mankind out of the Garden of Eden (Paradise) written by John Milton in 1667.

GLOSSARY

Laertes   in Shakespeare's **Hamlet**, Laertes is the brother of Ophelia. He fights a fencing duel with Hamlet which turns fatal (V.ii).

a palpable hit   a touch which can be felt. Osric rules 'a very palpable hit' has been made by Hamlet on Laertes, in his role as umpire, or judge of the fencing match.

'Howzat'   call for umpire to recognise that someone is out of the game.

daughters of Lear   Goneril and Regan, and their younger sister Cordelia.

121 Tulse Hill . . . Upper Norwood areas in south London.

123 Tamp   onomatopoeic word, the pat or thud of tennis ball upon racket strings.

Aertex logo   the brand name of a sports shirt and its embroidered trademark.

sucklers   animals not yet weaned.

124 inter-uterine   inside the womb.

125 Anorexic   term used to describe people who avoid food, or have a severe lack of appetite, due to emotional problems. The condition, Anorexia Nervosa, leads sufferers to become extremely emaciated.

127 Jackson Pollock   American artist (1912–56). Developed a technique called 'action painting' which involved drips and splashes of paint.

the NME   a newspaper for music fans, the **New Musical Express**.

Beethoven   Ludwig van Beethoven, German composer (1770–1827).

Bartok   Bela Bartok, Hungarian composer (1881–1945).

Hungarian Dances   by Bartok. He was fond of traditional dance rhythms and folk songs and these influenced his own compositions.

Debussy   Claude Debussy, French composer (1862–1918). He wrote music which attempted to create pictures in sound, a kind of 'musical Impressionism'.

142

29 *amnion*   membrane around the embryo in the womb, it contains fluid which protects the unborn animal or child.

calf   young seal.

31 *caesium*   a soft alkaline metal.

Chernobyl   place in Ukraine where the worst nuclear disaster to date took place, 25–6 April 1986.

glasnost   literally 'speaking aloud' in Russian; the policy of openness initiated by President Gorbachev in the mid 1980s.

golau glas   blue light (Welsh: *golau* – light, pronounced roughly 'gol-e'; *glas* – blue).

33 *Georgia O'Keefe*   American painter (1887–1986). Her work eventually took on a surrealist feel.

34 *Lurcher*   dog which has distinct elements of greyhound in breeding (usually crossed with a collie).

Rhygyfarch   (pronounced 'Rur-ger-farch', with ch as in loch) a clerk of St David's (1056–99), hailed as the most learned Welshman of his time. He wrote a **Lament** for Wales.

Kells   Ceanannas Mor in Co. Meath in the Republic of Ireland. Famous for its monastery and the illuminated Book of Kells produced there *c.* 800.

milgi   greyhound (Welsh).

■ Technical terms

alliteration   the same sound repeated at the beginning of words
near to one another, which creates a sound effect, e.g.

> Sentiments in very vulgar verses . . .
> . . . ordering oysters or ironing . . .
> . . . something flimsy in a flatteringly wrong size . . .
>   'I Wouldn't Thank You for a Valentine', pages 32–3

ballad   a poem written in short regular *stanzas* which often tells a
story of tragedy or heroism. One of the features of the ballad is
often the inclusion of some dialogue. See 'Young Edgcumbe',
page 42.

figurative language   language that has more than one possible
meaning; language that is not literal.

first person   if the speaker of the poem is talking about him or
herself, using I, me (and we, us) then they are said to be speaking
in the first person. The poem 'Spring', page 63, is written in the
first person.

form   in poetry this usually means the arrangement of the lines; the
pattern of the poem; sometimes also the style in which the poem
is written.

free verse   poetry that doesn't follow any set patterns. It may or
may not have *rhyme* and its rhythm and line arrangement are
usually irregular, e.g.

> I like to watch my little sister
> playing hopscotch, admire the neat hops-and-skips of her,
> their quick peck,
> never-missing their mark, not
> over-stepping the line.
> She is competent at peever.
>   'Poem for My Sister', page 24

144

TECHNICAL TERMS

haiku   a Japanese *form* based on the number of *syllables* in a line, rather than on any *rhymes*. Lines 1 and 3 have five syllables, while line 2 has seven. Words are chosen carefully so that as much as possible can be said in such a brief space. See 'Haiku Moments', page 14 and 'Strugnell's Haiku', page 120.

image   a picture brought to mind by the words or phrases used and which can have a strong effect on the reader, e.g.

> She is arrow.
> At two miles a minute
> the pigeon bursts like a city.

'Peregrine Falcon', page 135

internal rhyme   where *rhyme* appears in the middle of lines (and occasionally within words), e.g.

> How mad I am, sad I am, glad that you won

'A Subaltern's Love-song', page 84

> And is that why your eye won't dry

'The Ballad of Charlotte Dymond', page 40

metaphor   a comparison where one thing is described as if it is the other (no need to use 'like' or 'as': see *simile*), e.g.

> Zinc sheets are kites

'Hurricane', page 13

> his eyes' ringed planets towing moons of ice

'Lurcher', page 134

> ***extended metaphor***   where the simple comparison is carried on to show how things are comparable in many ways, e.g. the description of the school as a ship in 'School at Four O'Clock', page 56.

monologue   a piece of writing which is meant to be spoken by one person. *Raps* are generally monologues and there are many other *forms*.

TECHNICAL TERMS

mood   often confused with *tone*, but easy to remember if you think of mood as the atmosphere evoked or the feeling that the reader is left with.

onomatopoeia   words which when spoken aloud have the same sound as the noise they describe, e.g. crack, boom, which add to the atmosphere of the writing, e.g.

> a first pianissimo slip of snow from the roof

'Musician', page 127

parody   an imitation of something else which usually makes fun of the original.

pastiche   a piece of writing made up of parts of other works. This is done to imitate style deliberately, often with the aim of making the original seem absurd. See 'A Christmas Carol', page 114.

quatrain   a *stanza* of four lines, usually with a regular *rhyme scheme*, e.g.

> I preen myself, I am a peacock word,
>   I am a call, am one
> Who does not need a tether or a cord,
>   I dally in the sun

'Ill Noun', page 93

rap   a rhythmic *monologue*, which usually has a musical background. See 'I Wouldn't Thank You for a Valentine', page 32.

renga   a sequence made up of linked *haiku* poems. See 'Study programme' page 151: 'Haiku Moments'.

rhyme   where the sounds of a word or of its final *syllable(s)* are echoed in another word nearby, e.g. chime/climb, away/clay, meaning/morning.

rhyme scheme   the pattern made by the *rhymes* at line endings. The way to mark out a rhyme scheme is to give a different letter to each different rhyme, e.g.

Encase your legs in nylons	a
Bestride your hills with pylons	a
O age without a soul;	b
Away with gentle willows	c
And all the elmy billows	c
That through your valleys roll.	b
Let's say good-bye to hedges	d
And roads with grassy edges	d
And winding country lanes;	e . . . etc.

'Inexpensive Progress', page 75

rhyming couplet   a pair of consecutive lines which *rhyme* with one another (and almost always the last two of the Shakespearian *sonnet form*), e.g.

Cold like a white root pressed in the bowels of earth
He looked, but also vulnerable – like birth.

'Lazarus', page 103

simile   a comparison in which one thing is said to be 'like' or 'as' another with elements in common, e.g.

the calf swam home *like* a salmon
furled in a waterfall

'The Vet', page 124

peas tight in their pods *as* sucklers

'Stealing Peas', page 123

sonnet   a form often used for love poems. It is always fourteen lines long with a regular *rhyme scheme*. See 'Strugnell's Sonnets', page 121.

sound patterns   this can include *rhyme* and also a number of other techniques used by poets to create more vivid effects, e.g. *onomatopoeia, alliteration.*

stanza   a verse; a group of lines.

subject matter   what the poem is about, e.g. my grandmother, six women.

syllable   a word, or part of it, like a beat in music, e.g. beaut-y (2), beaut-i-ful (3), beaut-i-ful-ly (4 syllables).

symbol   an *image* or thing which represents other things and ideas (as well as itself), e.g. a dove is often taken to be a symbol of peace.

syntax   the order of the words.

tercet   a *stanza* of three lines usually, although not always, with a regular *rhyme scheme*, e.g.

> That spring was late. We watched the sky
> and studied charts for shouldering isobars.
> Birds were late to pair. Crows drank from the lamb's eye.
>
> 'Neighbours', page 131

theme   the idea that lies behind the *subject matter*, e.g. old age, the treatment of old people, etc. A poet may write a number of poems on the same theme, yet each one will have a different subject matter.

tone   the easiest way to define this in terms of a poem is to think about the 'tone of voice' of the speaker in the poem (whether the poet or a character). Are they cheerful, playful, sarcastic, pessimistic . . . ?

villanelle   a fixed *form* made up of five *tercets* and a final *quatrain*, with a repeated pattern of whole lines. It was a very popular form in the Middle Ages and has been revived in the twentieth century. See 'Manifesto', page 117.

Study programme

This study programme is divided into three sections:

- In the first you will find that there are ideas for activities based on individual poems or small groups of poems usually by a single poet.
- The second offers ways of working thematically, combining poems from more than one poet at a time.
- The third section gives suggestions for general activities, using poems in any combination.

Section 1

James Berry

① *What We Said Sitting Making Fantasies*

Read this poem with a group of friends and then create a new fantasy each. Put together, these can form a new poem for performance to your class.

Write your poem up, add pictures to go with it and create a fantastic wall display.

② *Pair of Hands against Football*

Aiming to recreate the atmosphere of the match, prepare a large group or class choral reading of the poem. The rhythm should help you. Add actions if they are helpful.

Write the commentator's script in which he or she puts forward the case that this goalkeeper should be given the 'Man of the Match' award.

3 *Coming of the Sun*

In your own words describe all the effects that sunshine has on people in England, according to Berry's poem.

Other weather conditions will have different effects on people, and these will vary depending on the part of the world in which they live. Consider and discuss the likely effects of a thunder-storm in Scotland or a light shower over the Sahara Desert. Make a list of as many possible weather and place combinations as you can and then write your own poem – 'Coming of the . . . ' – about one combination from that list.

4 *Quick Ball Man*

In a group, one person can act as commentator and read the poem, while the rest mime the actions.

Create your own 'commentary' poem on a sports hero or hero-ine of your choice. Try using **rhyming couplets**, but if the poem feels wrong, change the pattern.

5 *Girls Can We Educate We Dads?*

When reading this poem, bear in mind what James Berry has to say:

> It's not necessary . . . for a non-West Indian speaker to try and read a Caribbean language and rhythm poem with the voice of a Caribbean person . . . When you read any . . . Caribbean-lan-guage-based poems . . . do feel out the rhythms. Feel it recreated. Then express it with your own easy natural voice.

In pairs improvise a conversation between Dad and daughter or son who wants to be more independent. How will Dad per-suade his child that he is not a 'chauvinist'?

6 *Double Act*

With a friend, prepare a paired reading of the poem, sharing out the lines carefully, particularly when you read the section beginning at line 17 ('And you said –').

Still with your partner, collaborate on a 'double act' poem of your own. Before you write, make notes and brainstorm ideas that will help you – think about what friendship means to you both, recall unusual incidents that you have enjoyed together and make the most of everyday activities as Berry does in his poem. Try to include a dialogue section, using the same format as Berry ('And you said . . . And I said . . . ').

7 *Hurricane*

What phrases and comparisons does Berry use to show the power of the wind?

Write a report of the hurricane's progress for a local newspaper. Consider carefully how its prose will differ from the style of the poem.

8 *Haiku Moments*

Examine the form of each of these three line poems carefully and check with the Glossary to make sure you understand how a *haiku* is structured. Using any of the ideas Berry includes (the rising sun – no. 8, a piece of fruit – no. 33, the sound of an instrument – no. 22, etc.) try out a haiku of your own.

Once you are confident with the haiku form you could try writing a sequence of them. One particular sequence of this type is called a *renga*: once you have written the first haiku, the second one must link by mentioning something from it. The third must link to the second, the fourth to the third, and so on. You can decide how many individual haiku verses to include but the very last one of the sequence should try to link ideas from *all* of the others.

9 *Mek Drum Talk, Man*

Work out a good, loud, rhythmic reading of this poem. Try to recreate the way in which Berry gives a vivid sense of the talking drums here.

Liz Lochhead

1 *What the Creature Said*

The poem is based on an incident in Mary Shelley's novel **Frankenstein**, when the creature (or monster) created by Dr Frankenstein comes upon the house of a blind man. Frankenstein's creation is usually thought of as evil and inhuman. What impression does the poem give of the creature?

With a partner take the roles of the blind man and his daughter. The man has had a visitor (remember that he cannot see) and is eager to tell his daughter about him. She in turn has heard that there is a strange and evil-looking creature on the loose. Act out their conversation.

2 *The Teachers*

In a group discuss Lochhead's experience of school and teachers. What differences are there between hers and your own? Interview older people for further comparisons.

Write a magazine article which deals with the changes in education over the last twenty/thirty/forty years. If this seems a large task, share aspects of the topic out between group members.

3 *Man on a Bench*

In spite of the brevity of this poem we can tell a great deal about the old man's personality. How does Lochhead achieve this?

4 *The Choosing*

Suppose that Mary also spotted Liz on the bus and tells her memories of all this in a different form, say in a conversation with her husband.

Write a story entitled 'The Choosing'.

5 *Poem for My Sister*

What reply would little sister make if she knew she was being talked about? With a partner improvise the conversation where the big sister gives advice and the smaller replies. What advice might a big brother give to a smaller one?

6 *Grandfather's Room* and *For My Grandmother Knitting*

Write down or act out the conversation that might take place between the grandfather and grandmother following a visit from their granddaughter.

7 *Poppies*

In groups dramatise this radio programme (and perhaps record it). Include an interview with the lady in high heels. Why did she disturb this solemn occasion?

Write the front page news on this incident.

8 *Riddle-Me-Ree*

This poem takes the form of a 'What am I?' riddle. The reader chooses a single letter from a word in each line to spell out a new word. The words from which the single letters are taken give extra clues to the 'identity'. Here's another one just to give you the idea:

> My first is in races, but never in seas;
> My second's in roads, but not found in trees.
> My third is in transport and also in pleasure.
> You'll find you will get there: just put these together.   [car]

With a partner write 'What am I?' riddles for these words – baby, radio, pet – or for some of your own choice.

Usually the answer to the riddle is given as a statement, but Liz Lochhead asks a question ('Is love the answer?'). Why does she do this?

9 *Wedding March*

Make a list of all the proverbs and clichés in this poem and find out where they came from originally. Add to them with any of your own and create a wall display or booklet on the use of English sayings.

Debate: This house believes that housework is still women's work.

10 *I Wouldn't Thank You for a Valentine*

Perform this *rap*, adding music and backing where you think it will fit.

Write some Valentine verse, genuine or jokey, either for cards or for the *Guardian* Personal Column. Display your work on big red hearts.

11 *Favourite Shade*

How does Lochhead get the reader to hear the Scots accent of the speaker in this *monologue*?

Draw some pictures to accompany this *rap* and/or perform it.

Charles Causley

1 *What Has Happened to Lulu?*

In a group discuss what might have happened to Lulu. Compare your theory with those of other groups, using evidence from the poem to support your ideas.

Compile a dossier on Lulu's disappearance, containing the following elements: the last day's entry from Lulu's diary; a reconstruction of the note (**stanza** 3); mother's reply to the questions; report by the investigating officer after interviews with mother, child and any further witnesses or relatives.

2 *The Ballad of Charlotte Dymond*

List the clues that led the constable to arrest Matthew Weeks for the murder.

Write Matthew's statement to the police and his final confession.

3 *Young Edgcumbe*

In a library, research the story of Richard III and the Princes in the Tower. Explain the connection between that story and the poem.

Either draw an eight-frame cartoon strip giving Edgcumbe's story (choosing captions and thought or speech bubbles from the **ballad**) or write the story of his exploits in the style of an historical chronicle.

4 *My Mother Saw a Dancing Bear*

The poem is almost like a child's story in style until the **tone** changes and we eventually reach a less than happy ending. If you were writing the story for a child would you change the ending? Explain your decision.

5 *I Saw a Jolly Hunter*

At first glance this poem seems like a simple nursery rhyme, yet it contains a serious statement on a controversial issue. What is the issue, and why do you think Causley uses this form for the statement?

Rewrite the story of the Jolly Hunter as a short fable in prose (a story with a moral or message: see Aesop's fables to help you with style and purpose).

6 *Richard Bartlett*

Explain
a) why some parts of this poem appear in italics
b) what you understand from the final line and a half.

Either write a full obituary for Richard Bartlett, or a detailed report of the accident, as it might appear in a modern local newspaper.

7 *Dick Lander*

Causley describes the way in which he and Sid teased this unfortunate man. Can you find any clues in the poem as to how he now feels about their youthful behaviour?

Imagine that Auntie learns what Sid and Charles are up to and challenges them in front of Uncle. In a group of four act out the situation.

8 *Six Women* and *Ward 14*

Who is the sixth woman in the ward? How do the poems relate to one another? If you have read other Causley poems before these two, look back and compare the style (*rhyme*, rhythm, *form*, etc.). Try to explain any differences you find.

With a partner improvise a conversation between Causley and the nurse who has been so sharp with his mother. Consider what he might want to take issue with over her treatment. How might the nurse react?

9 *Stang Hunt*

Explain how the poet brings out the fear and excitement of this event.

What do you think the last two lines of the poem mean?

10 *School at Four O'Clock*

What is the school compared with in the first **stanza** of this poem? What are the similarities between the two things which make this **extended metaphor** work?

Write in prose the thoughts that the teacher has about the school, his pupils and the education they receive.

11 *I Am the Song*

With a group discuss each line of the poem individually and say why each is surprising. Explain exactly what the poet has done. Is there an answer to who (or what) is speaking the verse?

Make up a group 'I am' poem using the same technique as Causley has. You could create a line or two each and then experiment with the best arrangement of them.

Grace Nichols

1 *Iguana Memory*, **Spring**, *On Her Way to Recovery*, **Hey There Now!** and **Conkers**

Study all these poems and write a brief and selective biography of Nichols's life from them.

2 *Be a Butterfly*

What does the preacher seem to mean about the butterfly and the caterpillar and why does Nichols finally say that he was right? Discuss your ideas with a partner.

3 *The Fat Black Woman Goes Shopping*

Draw a cartoon strip of the Fat Black Woman's shopping trip, using the words of the poem to caption it.

Write a letter to the problem page of a magazine – why are fashionable clothes only made in tiny sizes?

4 *Beauty*

Poets, artists and philosophers have always argued over the nature of beauty. You could look at John Keats's 'Ode on a Grecian Urn' as another poem about beauty, where he says 'Beauty is truth, truth beauty'. This sounds somewhat final, so why do poets continue to try to define beauty? Compare Keats's perspective with that of Nichols. Do they have anything in common?

Write your own poem called 'Beauty'.

5 *Abra-Cadabra*

Explain why the poem bears this title. What view of Nichols's mother is given to us here and what is her particular magic?

6 *Wha Me Mudder Do*

Read the poem aloud and put mimed actions to it.

Nichols wrote this poem in Caribbean Nation Language, a Creole dialect of English. If she decided to write it in Standard English prose, how would it be presented? Write that version, and then vote on which version your class prefers.

7 *Praise Song for My Mother*

Using the pattern of Nichols's poem (You were/ . . . to me/ . . . and . . . and . . . etc.) write a praise song for someone you know. Choose expressive and unusual **images**, comparisons and adjectives. What advice will the final line contain?

8 *Two Old Black Men on a Leicester Square Park Bench*

Stage an interview with these two men and let them tell you their dreams. Present your dramatisation to the class.

9 *On Receiving a Jamaican Postcard*

In a group prepare a reading of this poem, with music and actions if you wish. (See what James Berry has to say about reading Caribbean dialect on page 150 before you begin.)

Can you get to the bottom of how Nichols feels about the picture on the postcard?

John Betjeman

1 *Dilton Marsh Halt*

Compare this poem with 'Inexpensive Progress'. Which one offers more hope?

The Halt is to be closed! As a class, hold a public meeting. Some will need to take the roles of the railway authority's representatives while you try to persuade them to keep the Halt open.

2 *Harvest Hymn*

This poem originally appeared as a letter to **Farmer's Weekly**. (Why do you think Betjeman sent it to that magazine?) Write a reply, in letter form, from a farmer wishing to defend modern agricultural methods.

3 *Inexpensive Progress*

Begin by making a list of the things which Betjeman sees as threats to the countryside in this poem. Written in the 1960s, the poem still reflects concerns felt by some today. Survey your local and the national press for up-to-date examples.

Basing your ideas on what you have found, write a letter to an MP giving your views on either transport policy or planning application restrictions.

4️⃣ *The Village Inn*

Find the point where the rhythm of the poem changes. What is the effect on the reader? Why has Betjeman done this?

With a partner, prepare two contrasting sets of publicity materials for 'The Bear' — one for before the alterations, and one for afterwards. Include bar menus, forthcoming attractions list, etc. Think carefully about the kind of person you are trying to attract in each case.

5️⃣ *Slough*

Betjeman would never really have wanted a town to be bombed, but you could make a list of all the things about Slough that he resents. Is Slough significant, or is it a **symbol** for something else?

Fight back! You are members of Slough Town Council. Prepare a brochure for tourists, with the aim of attracting them to the town. (Use your local town as a model.)

6️⃣ *Cornish Cliffs*

Either find some pictures to illustrate the two contrasting landscapes of the poem, or, if you are artistic, sketch them yourself. What **moods** or atmospheres do they conjure up?

Write your own descriptive poem, contrasting two views of places you know. If you can use rhyming **tercets**, so much the better, but your poem can take any form.

7️⃣ *Hunter Trials*

What is Betjeman's attitude towards young competitive riders? How do the **rhyme**, rhythm and choice of vocabulary help make his view clear to the reader?

Illustrate any **stanza** of this poem. (Look out for Thelwell's drawings for ideas.)

8 A Subaltern's Love-song

Describe the feelings of the subaltern. How do the rhythm and **rhyme** of the poem help get these feelings across to the reader?

Write Miss Joan Hunter Dunn's diary, describing the events of the day from her point of view.

9 How to Get On in Society

Debate the motion: This house believes that the way in which we speak no longer makes any difference to our ability to get on in society.

10 Inland Waterway

Compare and contrast this poem with 'Inexpensive Progress' and 'Dilton Marsh Halt'.

11 Beaumaris, December 21, 1963

Look closely at the poem to discover how Betjeman introduces brightness and light to his descriptions.

Speak or write Laurelie Williams's thoughts as she stands, hands in the washing-up bowl, thinking back over the events.

12 Death in Leamington

Why does the poet spend so much detail on the old lady's surroundings at her death?

Prepare what the nurse will say to the lady's next of kin about how she found her, either as a speech or in writing.

Elizabeth Jennings

1 *Parts of Speech I–IV*

Check that you know how these parts of speech work in sentences.

Try out a poem called 'Pronoun', 'Article' or 'Conjunction'. How might these parts of speech describe themselves, their places in sentences and their relationships to other parts? If you find a poem too difficult, try a prose description, but remember to use the **first person**.

2 *A Question of Form*

Look through 'Technical terms' (pages 144–8) at some examples of **form**. With a partner decide which of these two statements is truer:

'The good/Work of art makes laws it must obey'

or

'poetry never should be cast/In form, but come without control'.

Are formal poems better than **free verse**? Compare your answers with the class or debate the ideas.

3 *The Enemies*

Who are the enemies and what is the motive for the invasion? These are questions left unanswered by the poem. Working in a group improvise and act out the invasion. Then produce a news bulletin for the TV news and present it to the class.

Write the story of the invasion as
a) an eyewitness account from someone in the city, or
b) the log of the invading commander.

4 *Old Woman*, *Old Man*, *My Grandmother* and *For My Mother*

Explore this group of poems with others, thinking about how Jennings conveys to us a sense of the age of her subjects and their feelings as they approach the end of their lives.

Compare the poet's reactions and emotions on the deaths of her mother and grandmother. Explain the differences, using the poems to support your observations.

Carefully describe the feelings of an elderly person in any form you think appropriate (diary, letter, **monologue**, etc.). You can base your writing on your knowledge of someone, not necessarily a relative.

5 *Song at the Beginning of Autumn* and *The Smell of Chrysanthemums*

Compare these two poems. What similarities are there in **form**, **subject matter**, **theme**, **mood**, **tone**, and handling between them? Give your answer in essay or oral form.

6 *Lazarus*

Read the original story of Lazarus in the Bible (John 11:1–44) making notes on extra details found there.

You are a news reporter with a notebook of facts and an interview you have conducted with an eyewitness (the poem). Write a front page scoop of the miraculous event. Explore in an editorial what the significance of the event seems to be to those who witnessed it.

7 *Love Poem*

Do you agree with Jennings's assessment of love? Reply to her in letter or poem form.

8 *An Age of Doubt*

Read each of the poems mentioned by Jennings here (see Glossary for details) and discuss them with others. How do you think the poems helped her

a) to begin to write better poetry, and

b) to lose her doubts?

Wendy Cope

1 *Tich Miller, Lizzy* and *Names*

Give each one of these girls or women the chance to tell their autobiographies for themselves. How do they feel about their experiences and the treatment they have received from others? Choose an appropriate form to present their stories whether oral (conversation, **monologue**) or written (letter, diary, etc.).

2 *For My Sister, Emigrating*

Read this poem in conjunction with Liz Lochhead's 'Poem for My Sister'.

3 *Engineers' Corner*

Decide with a partner how one could describe the **tone** of this poem.

Find out the names of as many writers buried in Westminster Abbey as you can. Then compile a list of famous engineers who might lie in Engineers' Corner. You could also invent a corner for other professions, justifying its existence (in verse if possible).

4 *Does She Like Word-Games?*

The poem is a word-game. In a group work out the rules of the game and then play it.

Produce your own word-game poems using these rules – He likes . . . but he doesn't like . . . *or* We love . . . but we can't abide . . . – or if you wish invent a completely new set of rules and try your poem out on other members of the group.

5 *A Christmas Carol, 19th Christmas Poem* and *Manifesto*

The first poem is a **pastiche** made up of parts of well-known carols. Notice the **rhyme scheme** and the **internal rhyme** and then try to create your own 'found' poem from bits taken from other sources. You could use carols or pop songs, country and western songs, skipping rhymes, advertising jingles, etc. Select interesting lines or phrases from your chosen source (they need not be well-known) and then assemble them, like a word jigsaw puzzle, to form a new poem. Some clever choices and assembly should lead to a poem that makes perfect sense.

The second poem uses the rhythm and **rhymes** of nursery rhyme. What is the effect of this?

For the third poem, in a large group (up to twelve or thirteen members) practise a reading of this poem with actions. The deliberately repeated lines will help you in arranging this.

'Manifesto' is written in a very old form called a **villanelle**. Perhaps your group could attempt one of your own.

Looking at all three poems together, what can you say about the way Wendy Cope approaches the writing of poetry?

6 *A Nursery Rhyme*

This is a **parody** of William Wordsworth's style. Ask your teacher to recommend some of his poems for comparison.

You could try rewriting other nursery rhymes in modern style and language, perhaps in the style of a particular newspaper, or turn them into **raps**.

7 *The Cricketing Versions*

Look up the Shakespeare references mentioned here and act them out as a group – **Hamlet** V.ii.239–324: 'Come, Hamlet, come and take this hand from me' to 'The drink, the drink; I am poison'd' and **King Lear** I.i.35–131: 'Attend the Lords of France' to 'which she calls plainness, marry her'. When you are happy with what is happening, omit the words and mime only the actions. Next, produce a sporting commentary to go with the actions. It need not be cricket. You could use tennis, rugby, etc. Present your 'sporting version' to the class and ask them to evaluate it.

If you are feeling very ambitious, Milton's **Paradise Lost** Book I might also inspire you.

8 *Strugnell's Haiku*

The **haiku** is a Japanese poetic form which relies on the number of **syllables** for its shape. Cope is pretending to write here as a struggling poet, Jason Strugnell. He has a lot of failings but he does have a good try at different forms of poetry. The effect is one of **parody**. However, you too could try some serious haiku, but don't be tempted to think they are easy to write just because the form looks simple (see 'Technical terms')!

9 *Strugnell's Sonnets (iv)* and *(vi)*

Both **sonnets** are **parodies** of ones written by William Shakespeare (numbers LV and CXVI). Read them and compare the attitudes towards love expressed by
a) Shakespeare
b) the invented struggling poet, Jason Strugnell
c) Wendy Cope.

The sonnet is a very rigorous form, but if you are feeling ambitious you could try to produce one on your own view of love or about a loved one.

Gillian Clarke

1 *Stealing Peas*

Discuss with a partner how the atmosphere of secrecy is created in this poem.

Rewrite the anecdote, in prose or poetry, as if the boy is telling it.

2 *The Vet* and *Anorexic*

Compare these two poems with 'Musician' as vivid memories from the poet's past. What can you tell about her age at the time of each event, and about her feelings as an adult looking back?

Write a thank-you letter from niece to aunt following one such stay, or the child's diary in prose following the birth of the calf.

3 *Musician*

Read the poem aloud, or record yourself reading it. Listen to it carefully to find examples of **onomatopoeia** and **alliteration**. Which parts of the poem sound like either the music itself, or any other sounds described?

Write a pen portrait, in prose or poetry, of a person whose habits and hobbies you remember.

4 *Swimming with Seals*

Look out for **alliteration** in this poem. Find as many examples as you can, then read the poem aloud several times. How does the sound of the poem add to the sense of what is happening in it?

Describe the event from the point of view of the watchers rather than the swimmers.

5 *No Hands*

Clarke does not seem to approve of the activities of these trainee fighter pilots. How does she interpret their actions and why might she object?

Hot seat either a fighter pilot commander or a representative from the Ministry of Defence about what is going on, and why these planes fly so low. Don't forget that the person in the hot seat has the right to reply in full.

6 *Lament*

A lament is a song which mourns a loss. Discuss the selection of things and people over whom the poet chooses to lament. Make a large poster to illustrate the poet's environmental (or other) concerns.

7 *Neighbours*

Find out what you can about what happened at Chernobyl in 1986 and explain its significance to the poem.

Is Clarke's poem optimistic or pessimistic? Explain to a partner which view you hold.

8 *My Box*

This poem is similar to many riddles in which you have to guess what the person is really talking about underneath the obvious descriptions. If we suppose that this poem is not about a box at all, what might the box represent? A closer look at its parts and contents might help you decide. Discuss the possibilities with others.

Write a poem about your own box – its contents will be personal to you.

9 *Red Poppy*

The poppy is described here in a number of ways. Which **stanza** contains, for you, the most effective **metaphor** for the poppy? Compare your view with that of others.

Choose another object, perhaps a flower, and write a three-line stanza describing it, using a **simile** or metaphor if you can. Pass your writing on to another person who should add their own **tercet** on the same topic, and so on until you have a group poem.

10 *Lurcher*

Read this poem as a group with 'Red Poppy' and 'Peregrine Falcon', and make a study of Clarke's use of imagery and **figurative language**. You could present this as an essay or as a radio programme with poetry readings.

11 *Peregrine Falcon*

How vivid do you find this description of the falcon?

Stanza 4 contains a startling **simile**. What effect does it create? Begin a collection of similes, verbal and visual, to discuss and display.

Section 2

In this section you will find some lists of poems which can be discussed and written about together because they are linked by a theme or an idea. These lists are not exhaustive, and are intended to get you thinking about how poems can be associated with one another. You will want to add to them from the poems in the anthology, choosing poems or poets that you particularly admire. The lists are followed by some suggestions for how to work with thematic groups of poems.

Mothers and daughters

Favourite Shade (Lochhead)
What Has Happened to Lulu? (Causley)
Abra-Cadabra; Wha Me Mudder Do; Praise Song for My Mother;
   On Her Way to Recovery; Hey There Now! (Nichols)
My Grandmother; For My Mother (Jennings)

Humans and animals

My Mother Saw a Dancing Bear; I Saw a Jolly Hunter (Causley)
Iguana Memory (Nichols)
Swimming with Seals; Peregrine Falcon (Clarke)

Making a fuss

Wedding March (Lochhead)
I Saw a Jolly Hunter (Causley)
The Fat Black Woman Goes Shopping (Nichols)
Inexpensive Progress; The Village Inn; Slough (Betjeman)
No Hands; Neighbours (Clarke)

Portraits of people

Quick Ball Man; Double Act (Berry)
Man on a Bench (Lochhead)
Richard Bartlett; Dick Lander; Six Women (Causley)
Two Old Black Men on a Leicester Square Park Bench (Nichols)
Death in Leamington (Betjeman)
Old Woman; Old Man (Jennings)
Tich Miller; Lizzy (Cope)
Anorexic; Musician (Clarke)

Old world/new world

Hurricane; Mek Drum Talk, Man (Berry)
My Mother Saw a Dancing Bear; Stang Hunt (Causley)
Iguana Memory; Conkers (Nichols)
The Village Inn (Betjeman)

Humour

I Wouldn't Thank You for a Valentine (Lochhead)
Hunter Trials; How to Get On in Society (Betjeman)
Engineers' Corner; A Christmas Carol; The Cricketing Versions
    (Cope)

Childhood experiences

What We Said Sitting Making Fantasies; Double Act (Berry)
The Teachers; The Choosing (Lochhead)
Dick Lander; Stang Hunt (Causley)
Iguana Memory; Be a Butterfly (Nichols)
Tich Miller (Cope)
Stealing Peas; The Vet (Clarke)

Beginnings and endings

The Ballad of Charlotte Dymond; Richard Bartlett; Ward 14
    (Causley)
Spring (Nichols)
Dilton Marsh Halt; Death in Leamington (Betjeman)
Song at the Beginning of Autumn (Jennings)
The Vet; Swimming with Seals (Clarke)

The poet's craft

A Question of Form (Jennings)
19th Christmas Poem; Manifesto (Cope)

1. Create a list of your own based on a single theme. A few ideas might be
   - Hopes and fears
   - Being different
   - Memories
   - People speaking aloud
   - Relationships
   - Love
   - Rites and rituals
   - Landscapes

   The list could go on – add your own ideas to it.

2. Make a group or class anthology based on a theme. Choose the poems carefully. Illustrate them. Gather together examples of your own poems on the same theme. Include prose writing (your own or that you have researched) which explores the theme in other ways.

   Your anthology could take the form of a book or a display.

3. Use the material you have collected for an anthology in a different way altogether. Produce a 'magazine' programme for radio or video. This will give you the opportunity to read and perform poems as well as present them visually.

4. Make a very selective choice of themes and poets. You could take just three poets and two or three poems from each which comment on a single theme. For instance, how do Wendy Cope, Liz Lochhead and Elizabeth Jennings deal with the theme of love in their poetry? Do they all define love in the same way? What differences are noticeable in their attitudes to it? How do the forms they write in tell us more about their approach to the subject matter? There are lots of comparisons that can be made between the handling of themes and ideas by different poets. A study of this kind would make an excellent literary essay, particularly if you used quotations to prove your findings.

Section 3

This section contains further ideas for exploring and enjoying the poems in this anthology and elsewhere.

☐ To carry out a single poet study you could concentrate on just the poems printed in this book. However, you might want to extend your study. The sections entitled 'About the poet' give some biographical details for each poet here, but you could research further and then decide whether the poetry is autobiographical in nature. You could look out for some of their other published works and find other poems. These could be presented to your group or class. Whenever you choose a new poem for others to hear, remember to explain to them why you chose it and what it is about the poem that particularly impresses you. Ask for others to give feedback on your choice – they may throw new light on what you are doing.

You could present your poet study in oral (live, radio, video) form or in writing (booklet, wall display, essay, magazine). Display it as a feature in your school library.

2 Produce a class anthology of your own poems inspired by a single poet. Publish it, or read your poems in an assembly. Don't forget to introduce your source of inspiration too.

3 Make a collection of advertising slogans. Group them according to the poetic techniques they use (rhyme, alliteration, etc.). Are there any which actually use quotations directly from poetry? Why do they do this? Present your findings to your own class, or to another one.

4 Make a collection of proverbs or adages or clichés and treat them as above. You could also
   a) look for references to any of the examples you have found in the poems of the anthology, or
   b) rewrite them, trying to make them more effective or unusual.

Longman Literature

Series editor: Roy Blatchford

Plays

Alan Ayckbourn   *Absurd Person Singular*   0 582 06020 6
Ad de Bont   *Mirad: A Boy from Bosnia*   0 582 24949 X
Oliver Goldsmith   *She Stoops to Conquer*   0 582 25397 7
Henrik Ibsen   *The Doll's House, Ghosts and The Wild Duck*   0 582 24948 1
Ben Jonson   *Volpone*   0 582 25408 6
Christopher Marlowe   *Doctor Faustus*   0 582 25409 4
Arthur Miller   *An Enemy of the People*   0 582 09717 7
J B Priestley   *An Inspector Calls*   0 582 06012 5
Terence Rattigan   *The Winslow Boy*   0 582 06019 2
Jack Rosenthal   *Wide-Eyed and Legless*   0 582 24950 3
Willy Russell   *Educating Rita*   0 582 06013 3
               Shirley Valentine   0 582 08173 4
Peter Shaffer   *Equus*   0 582 09712 6
               The Royal Hunt of the Sun   0 582 06014 1
Bernard Shaw   *Arms and the Man*   0 582 07785 0
               The Devil's Disciple   0 582 25410 8
               Pygmalion   0 582 06015 X
               Saint Joan   0 582 07786 9
R B Sheridan   *The Rivals and The School for Scandal*   0 582 25396 9
Oscar Wilde   *The Importance of Being Earnest*   0 582 07784 2

Longman Literature Shakespeare

Series editor: Roy Blatchford

A Midsummer Night's Dream   0 582 08833 X (paper)
                           0 582 24590 7 (cased)
As You Like It   0 582 23661 4 (paper)
Hamlet   0 582 09720 7 (paper)
Henry IV Part I   0 582 23660 6 (paper)
Henry V   0 582 22584 1 (paper)
Julius Caesar   0 582 08828 3 (paper)
                0 582 24589 3 (cased)
King Lear   0 582 09718 5 (paper)
Macbeth   0 582 08827 5 (paper)
            0 582 24592 3 (cased)
The Merchant of Venice   0 582 08835 6 (paper)
                        0 582 24593 1 (cased)
Othello   0 582 09719 3 (paper)
Richard III   0 582 23663 0 (paper)
Romeo and Juliet   0 582 08836 4 (paper)
                   0 582 24591 5 (cased)
The Tempest   0 582 22583 3 (paper)
Twelfth Night   0 582 08834 8 (paper)

Longman Group Limited,
Longman House, Burnt Mill, Harlow,
Essex, CM20 2JE, England
and Associated Companies throughout the world.

First published 1995
ISBN 0 582 25400 0

Editorial material set in 10/12pt Gill Sans Light
Produced by Longman Singapore Publishers (Pte) Ltd
Printed in Singapore

Consultants: Geoff Barton and Jackie Head

Acknowledgements

We are grateful to the following copyright holders for permission to
reproduce poems:

The author's agent, on behalf of the author James Berry for 'Coming of the Sun', 'Double Act'
& 'Haiku Moments'; Carcanet Press Ltd for 'Musician', 'Anorexic', 'The Vet', 'Swimming with Seals',
'Lurcher', 'Lament', 'No Hands' & 'Stealing Peas' from The King of Britain's Daughter by Gillian Clarke
(1993) & 'Neighbours', 'My Box', 'Red Poppy' & 'Peregrine Falcon' from Letting in the Rumour by Gillian
Clarke (1989);

'Song at the Beginning of Autumn'	© 1955 Elizabeth Jennings
'Old Woman'	© 1958 Elizabeth Jennings
'Old Man'	© 1958 Elizabeth Jennings
'The Enemies'	© 1955 Elizabeth Jennings
'My Grandmother'	© 1961 Elizabeth Jennings
'Love Poem'	© 1966 Elizabeth Jennings
'Lazarus'	© 1961 Elizabeth Jennings
'Parts of Speech'	© 1992 Elizabeth Jennings
'A Question of Form'	© 1992 Elizabeth Jennings
'An Age of Doubt'	© 1992 Elizabeth Jennings
'For My Mother'	© 1992 Elizabeth Jennings
'The Smell of Chrysanthemums'	© 1992 Elizabeth Jennings

Elizabeth Jennings has asserted her moral right to be identified as the author of the above
poems in accordance with sections 77 and 78 of the Copyright, Designs and Patents Act
1988.

Faber and Faber Ltd for 'A Nursery Rhyme', 'Tich Miller', 'Engineers' Corner', 'Strugnell's Sonnets (IV)
(VI)', 'Manifesto' & 'Strugnell's Haiku (I) (II) (III)' from Making Cocoa for Kingsley Amis by Wendy Cope
(1986), 'The Cricketing Versions', 'Does She Like Word-Games?', 'For My Sister, Emigrating', '19th
Christmas Poem' & 'Names' from Serious Concerns by Wendy Cope (1992), 'A Christmas Carol' &
'Lizzy' from Does She Like Word-Games? by Wendy Cope (Anvil Press Ltd 1988);

The Ballad of Charlotte Dymond'	© 1992 Charles Causley
'School at Four O'Clock'	© 1992 Charles Causley
'Young Edgoumbe'	© 1992 Charles Causley
'I Saw A Jolly Hunter'	© 1970 Charles Causley
'What Has Happened to Lulu?'	© 1970 Charles Causley
'My Mother Saw a Dancing Bear'	© 1970 Charles Causley